"I have been sent several products lately. Most I did not endorse as they were simply fluff when it came to Facebook marketing for home businesses. Jim and Brian's new book was a really great surprise. I was stunned at the precise tactics and strategies that were in there—many I had never seen before. This book, I predict, will become a classic in the home business social media arena. A MUST-READ for anyone who is serious about their network marketing business utilizing social media and Facebook for massive success! BRILLIANT!"
- Doug Firebaugh, 29-year veteran of network marketing producing hundreds of millions in sales

-

"While everyone is jumping on the social media band wagon, afraid of missing the boat on this extraordinary new tool that can revolutionize their business, very few—especially in the direct selling industry—fully grasp its strategic integration and successful tactical implementation. The insights on the strategic alignment of the key sales goals using a tailored-made Social Media (SM) plan are extremely helpful in this book, both for the independent distributor to increase her activity and SM ROI as well as for corporate to carefully play and monitor the SM KPIs for optimal results. A very useful strategic and implementation guideline much needed for our industry."
- Mona Ameli, recognized as 1 of the 20 most influential women in the direct selling industry by Direct Selling News

-

"Jim Lupkin and Brian Carter provide valuable information and practical techniques for direct sellers that will help them use Facebook more effectively in their businesses."
- Debbie Squier, 15-year veteran of network marketing and direct selling executive recruiter

"When I think of an expert in marketing through Facebook, I think first of Jim Lupkin. Jim has been a source of education, coaching and expertise for several years. This book will be a valuable resource for those of us who know our products and services but haven't yet learned how to optimize the Internet as a marketing device. I would recommend it to my fellow learners."
- Garry Ford, former Chairman of the Direct Sellers Association of Canada and 37 year veteran of network marketing

"This new book by Jim Lupkin and Brian Carter is full of very practical tips that will help you to immediately leverage the power of Facebook to grow your organization/business. They show you things that actually get results, not theory ... real-world stuff that matters. Expect immediate results from these proven techniques!"
- Cindy & Kirby Wright, 25-year veterans of network marketing and million dollar income earners

"Jim Lupkin's new book is quickly going to become a successful network marketer's best friend! What I love about this new book is the step-by-step, practical advice that everyone can implement and start getting results within days. You even get suggestions about what to write, word by word! It is so important to learn to use the social media in an appropriate way, and in this way you will be able to magnify the results in your business. I am in total alignment with Jim's teachings about using our offline skills to build real friendships first and, only then, approach people about our opportunity! If you want success in network marketing, this book can be your short-cut!"
- Masa Cemazar & Miguel Montero, million dollar income earners of network marketing spanning business across 30 countries on 5 continents

"This is a must-read book for everyone who is looking to build a business successfully using social media, especially Facebook. Jim Lupkin is one of the best who understands the social and commerce side of a business. I would recommend this book."
- Evan Klassen, best selling author and entrepreneur

-

"There are many books on how to build your direct sales business face to face, but this is the foremost authority on how to build it on Facebook. What I appreciated most about this book was the depth of experience brought by the authors. They mastered in practice what they are now teaching in this book. A must-read for anyone determined to build a successful direct sales business."
- David Rutz, 20-year veteran of network marketing who built 2 organizations in excess of 80,000 distributors

-

"I have known Jim Lupkin for over a decade and have had the pleasure of using his services on more than one occasion. I have always found Jim to be honest, professional and willing to go the extra mile to keep his clients satisfied. Jim is very skilled with technology and patient with those who are not. It is very fitting that he would write a book on social media, particularly for this industry. Jim is the ultimate networker who knows the value of using technology to the benefit of building success. His writing style makes it easy to apply that which he instructs in his book."
- Carol Ford, business development specialist

"I met Jim Lupkin through social media in 2003. In 2006, we met face to face in Ahmedabad, India, for a convention in IT Gujarat, the silicon valley of India. Because of his social media teachings, I have been able to grow my business in Malaysia, Singapore, Thailand, Indonesia, Hong Kong, Macau, India, China and the US. I highly recommend this book for those who want an international business."

- Dr. Tom Academia Jr., professional network marketer in the Philippines

-

"Finally, a book that sheds the light on how to properly build a business online! Jim has done a great job pulling together the keys to online success. And, he has presented them through the eyes of successful business owners. All of the strategies described have been proven. They are clear, simple and actionable. When you follow these strategies, you will have put yourself on the road to success—with a global reach, no less."

- Dorina Lanza, 23 year veteran of network marketing and named one of the "Best Trainers in Network Marketing" by the editors of MLM Insider

-

"I absolutely loved how this book is step-by-step for direct sales and network marketing business owners. It is geared to go through each step with not only the "how to" guide, but it gives explanation of why it will help a business owner's online marketing strategy. This type of book could be so priceless to a business owner's success. Getting set up online immediately can be a game changer for people in this industry, and this book is key to helping consultants do just that. Not only will people be able to follow the steps, they will be able to continue to grow, knowing what to do next. It's just what the industry ordered."

- Jill McCarthy, 6 figure income earner in 2 network marketing companies

Network Marketing For Facebook

Proven Social Media Techniques For Direct Sales & MLM Success

JIM LUPKIN & BRIAN CARTER

ISBN: 978-1-887938-24-2

DEDICATION

This book is dedicated to every network marketing professional, no matter what level of success. To the ones who struggle, we hope this book gives you the courage to never give up and a clear path to reach your potential. To the ones who have seen success, we applaud you. You have overcome obstacles and barriers and paved the road for others to follow. This book is for you to share with your team, so they, too, can succeed in a time where building relationships around the world has never been easier because of Facebook. **Most importantly, thank you for daring to dream of a life beyond the cubicle!**

CONTENTS

ACKNOWLEDGMENTS

From Jim Lupkin

I believe a beautiful life can only be achieved with God by your side. Thank you, God, for being my perseverance over the last 19 years with my network marketing and social media career that led me to write this book.

My nanny always said, "Jimmy, one day you are going to change the world." Thank you, Nanny, for believing in me when, at times, I didn't believe in myself. I know you are smiling down from heaven. Maybe this book will change the lives of a few people, thus changing the world.

My mom never hesitated to help me, no matter the cost. Thank you, Mom, for helping me get my start by giving me $495 to become a distributor in my first network marketing company in 1995. I know it was your entire life savings at the time.

My dad always inspired me to keep going, no matter how bad the failure. He always said, "Just keep going. You'll make it. It might not be this business or this year. You'll get there eventually, if you don't quit." Thank you, Dad, for being an inspiration when I needed it most.

My wife was the only person who could get me to balance my life between business and personal. Thank you, Marianne, for opening my eyes to the importance of family and enjoying life outside of business. I am a better person because of it. And double thanks to her for serving as copy editor for this book!

My daughter was born at a time when I settled into mediocrity. She gave me the strength to stretch out of my comfort zone and go for my dreams. Thank you, Jade. I love you. I pray one day I can return the favor by being your inspiration that you, too, can live your dreams.

My son is only six months old. My wife and I are full-time, stay-at-home parents, and it has given us a different lifestyle with him. We get to see him grow up. This experience inspires me to help every distributor experience the same. Thank you, Mason, for making my days interesting.

My friends and family have taught me a lot about life. Even in the most frustrating of experiences, I came out a better person. Thanks to all of you for being a part of my journey to discovering myself and why I am here on this Earth.

Over my 19-year career, I have met thousands of leaders in network marketing. Thank you for being a guiding light to millions of people who join network marketing for a better life. And to all the distributors, your passion to do better with your life encourages me to keep moving forward.

From Brian Carter

It's always a huge learning experience writing a book, no matter what size. So thanks to whoever created books in the first place and all the people who buy them, even though many of those people don't actually read them.

I want to thank Jim because he's the network marketing expert. I'm a digital marketing and social media guy. I'm glad he brought me into this project. I have enjoyed learning more about the industry and met some phenomenal people. I want to thank our great interviewees. What I come away with is that there are some very clear dos and don'ts in this industry. One of the biggest takeaways is that it's very similar to social media as a whole: it's all about the people.

And of course, thanks to God, my family and all the amazing people I've met in business!

Need more than reading a book? Bring the book to life with diagrams and how-to videos. Stay current with the latest social media strategies and how they can grow your business by joining our community: http://socialmediadirectsales.com/training

Want personal, one-on-one coaching? Go here: http://socialmediadirectsales.com/coaching

1. Our Success Is Now Your Success

What will you gain from reading this book?

You will never run out of people to speak with about your business.

You will be able to build trusted long-term relationships that lead to more customers, distributors and referrals.

It won't be easy, yet it won't be hard. Like everything in life, it will be a battle you fight and win from within. Will you commit to our training? Will you be humble and allow us to coach you? Will you be disciplined enough to work until you achieve your financial goal with your network marketing company? If you answered yes to all three questions, then the next success we want to achieve in our journey is YOURS.

The Authors' Stories

So, before you spend 20,000 words with Jim Lupkin and Brian Carter, shouldn't you find out who they are?

Jim Lupkin

If you ask around, some might call me crazy. Some might call me a workaholic. Some might call me an entrepreneur or a social media guru. I think I am just a simple man who loves to make new friends using the Internet.

If you are anything like me, you want to know that the person who is teaching and coaching you has already succeeded in what you're trying to do with your life. Before we start your step-by-step Facebook training, let me share my story and why I decided to write this book.

Like you, I didn't want a job to dictate how much I was worth. I also didn't want to miss out on life because I spent most of my time stuck in an office. These two reasons are what attracted me to network marketing at the age of 18.

I was introduced to network marketing by my father's friend, Randy. He was a local businessman. My father thought it would be a good idea to check out network marketing since I wanted to own my own business. In October of 1995, I attended my first business opportunity meeting at a hotel for a company. I was overwhelmed with excitement because I was about to become an entrepreneur! As I walked into the conference, I noticed several hundred people. Many were school teachers from my school. Seeing these people gave me confidence that maybe this was a real opportunity to achieve my dreams. They treated me as an equal and not a student. This made me feel confident because now I was hanging with some of the most respected people in our community, not a bunch of my peers who only thought about partying and having fun. The most memorable moment, for me, was meeting the speaker. He was in shape and dressed well, had a beautiful girl by his side, and he seemed to have it all together. I wanted to be just like him.

At the end of the night, the speaker got into his shiny, silver Lexus. I jumped into my 1982 Nissan Maxima. When I pushed hard on the gas, the Maxima would engulf the cars behind me in a huge, black cloud of diesel smoke. Needless to say, I felt bad for any cars behind me. I raced home to tell my family what just happened and asked them if I could borrow $495.00 to sign up as a distributor.

I might as well have asked for a million dollars. I was 18 years old and still in high school. I had no job. My family was poor. I lived with my mother, grandmother, aunt and two cousins in a two-bedroom home. In my younger years, we slept three to a bed. We shopped at The Salvation Army, lived on welfare and ate mayo or syrup sandwiches for most meals. Though we didn't have much, I had an amazing childhood. My two cousins were like my brother and sister, my grandmother loved us like we were her own children, and my mother had a zest for life. We were a close family. Though I didn't live with my father and we hadn't established a relationship until I was 14 years old, he became my biggest cheerleader from a distance, rooting me on to follow my dreams.

My mom gave me the money from her hidden cookie jar stash and said, "Go and fulfill your dreams. I love you." I will be forever grateful she gave me what little money she had saved so that I could start my journey.

I was eager to get started. Randy took me to a training event where the most successful distributors taught the proper way to build the business, which is how all companies still train today. You know the routine. You start by making a list of everyone you know and pitch your business to them. It might work for some people, but as a high school student, my list consisted of the peers I sat with at lunch. I struggled with my list for the first four months.

Then, in the winter of 1996, everything changed. Our librarian taught us how to use the Internet. While we were learning, I found AOL groups. They were categorized by interests. One interest was Small Business. I spent the next three years in that group and many other groups, making friends with people all around the world. Ultimately, it led me to sponsor 40 new distributors within 36 months. No longer was I limited by my circumstances. I now consider my first attempt in network marketing to be a success, even though it didn't make me wealthy. It opened my eyes to what we now call social media.

Three years later, I went to college in Rhode Island. I double majored in Entrepreneurship and Finance, hoping one day to be a successful entrepreneur. Just when I thought my network marketing career was behind me, I received an unexpected phone call in 2001. A friend from my first company asked if I wanted to join a new company. I was too focused on my college studies to give it much thought, but he wouldn't give up on me. After months of trying, he left me the voicemail that changed my network marketing career, taking me from amateur to professional. He asked if I had an interest in working personally with one of the most successful distributors of all time, Mark Yarnell. I had read this guy's book ten times. He was a best-selling author on network marketing and had grown a team to 300,000 distributors around the world. Of course I'd work with him! If I could learn from this network marketing guru and combine that with my understanding of social media, I knew I would succeed in the way I had always dreamt. In April 2001, I became a distributor in my next network marketing company.

For the next three years, I went to college full time, worked part time, followed Mark Yarnell's teachings and worked on my social media skills. With much trial and error, I learned that traditional paid advertising is not as effective as building trusted online relationships. My hard work was starting to pay off; in my first year, I signed up an average of four new distributors a month. In my second year I averaged seven, and by my third year, I was signing up 30 new distributors each month. Even more thrilling, 40 percent of the top recruiters in the company were on my team. My team and I created millions of dollars in sales for the company.

It was difficult for me to enjoy all this success when I saw hundreds of families struggle and even lose their life savings in network marketing by falling for gimmicks that promised to help them succeed. One woman who lost her life savings, Annette, was a dear friend of mine. I wish I could have helped her, but I found out too late. She was in her late 70's when we met, and she had an amazing outlook on life. I would have loved to have her as a grandmother. She wanted to be free to spend all of her time enjoying family and seeing the world.

She was drawn into network marketing because of the promise of time freedom and big money. She spent all of her life savings trying to be successful in network marketing, working with marketers who promised to help her. In her mid-80's, after losing her savings, she ended up going back to work at a grocery store. Her husband passed away soon after, as well.

I was outraged because all they wanted to do was fulfill the network marketing dream. They were taken advantage of by people who promoted flashy marketing gimmicks. Today, these marketing gimmicks are hidden behind the guys promising to give you Facebook tricks to build a downline (the group of distributors you find, convert and train, and from whose sales you also receive a percentage) fast for only $50.00 a month, access to secret Facebook tools to explode your customer base for only $497.00 and the list goes on. Don't be fooled. Building relationships is your only way to success in network marketing.

Even though my team and I had success, the Internet was still in its infancy stage. There weren't enough people online or ways to easily connect with them. If I was in an AOL group with 212 members, I couldn't teach 100 distributors to talk to the same people. This wouldn't be a problem for long because the Internet would continue to grow significantly year after year.

In 2004, I spent time figuring out how to build better technology and bring together more people online. My friends who lost money became the driving force behind me wanting to find a better way. I interviewed and spent time with dozens of network marketing companies, distributors and technology vendors in the industry. By end of the year, I realized I lacked the technology skills to create an effective process. What do all entrepreneurs do at this point? Get educated!

Two years later, I contacted my friend, Chetan, who owned a promising software company in India. I had met him through a Yahoo Chat group years earlier. I offered to help him run his company so he could focus on software development. In return, he would teach me everything he knew about software. He was hesitant because I lacked the understanding of software development. I told him I would prove myself by generating $50,000 in product sales over the next 90 days. He agreed.

Not only did I achieve $50,000, I surpassed it by $30,000. All thanks to social media.

I spent the next two years learning everything I could about technology, and Chetan received over 1,000 new customers from my social media efforts. We captured a

$40,000 client, met a software developer owner from Arizona who sent us $160,000 in work over a six-month period and worked with network marketing companies in Malaysia, Philippines and Singapore through Myspace (the old Facebook).

In our third year, Chetan and I got aggressive and built our own social network to compete against Facebook and Myspace. It was a grueling nine months of writing code and designing hundreds of web pages with eighteen developers and four designers. Even though I didn't write any of the code, it was a wonderful experience to be part of the technology side of social media. Our website, Ojeez, was the 17,000th most visited website in the world out of millions, according to its Alexa rating (Alexa is a website that has ranked the most popular sites on the web since 1996). We had offers to sell out early, but I couldn't resist building the next big social network. It was a wonderful experience, but after a couple of years, Facebook was the clear winner in the social network war.

With four years of technology and thirteen years of network marketing and social media experience, I joined my third network marketing company. I was excited to put everything I learned to work. In four months we grew our team to 300+ distributors and $110,000 in product sales. The combination of technology, network marketing and social media know-how was working.

Toward the end of 2008, I attended the first social media event happening in the United States in Denver, Colorado. It took me 13 years to realize what I was doing online had a name. The speaker at the event called it "social media." I just saw it as making new friends online. At the end of the event, hundreds of people were still confused because the speaker did not teach them how to grow a business using it. I knew with my experience, I could coach and train entrepreneurs on how to grow their business. I started a consulting practice, working with network marketing professionals in various companies. I taught them how to build a network on sites like Facebook and, more importantly, how to generate sales.

Two years later, I relocated to Scottsdale, Arizona. Alongside Todd and Donna Newman, I co-launched Summa Social, an agency dedicated to small business and network marketing professionals. Over the next three years, we became one of the largest social media agencies in Arizona. We helped manage hundreds of small business owners and network marketing professionals with their social media accounts. We coached or trained more than 10,000 entrepreneurs. We had the opportunity to work with Mikel Harry, founder of Six Sigma and ForRent.com. Six Sigma helps companies maximize their efficiency and is used by more than two-thirds of the Fortune 500 companies. Six Sigma taught me to create simple systems that yield maximum success without making things complicated. ForRent.com is one of the largest websites online for apartment searches. ForRent.com taught me how to create success for many people at one time since we co-managed 4,000 of their apartment complexes using our social media technology.

In October 2012, my wife, Marianne, relocated to Scottsdale, Arizona. She wanted to be an entrepreneur without needing to raise a lot of money, open an office or hire employees, so she joined a network marketing company. Her team did $13,000 in product sales within 45 days using social media. It was a vigorous company, but her body didn't do well with their product.

A few months later, she joined a new company. Her team produced $23,000 in product sales during the first 30 days using social media. Though Marianne is not actively building that business today, the team continues to thrive within the company.

That same company also offered me the opportunity to be their Social Media Director. This position allowed me to put all of my experience from technology, network marketing and social media to the ultimate test by working with 40,000 distributors in multiple countries with a management team who thought about their distributors first. Over the next 17 months, the company grew its total sales from $11 million to more than $85 million. They are now recognized as the 100th largest network marketing company in the world, according to Direct Selling News. Working closely with Facebook-approved companies, Jim and Brian were able to validate that this company is one of the top network marketing companies on Facebook. More importantly, tens of thousands of distributors are having more success because they understand how to use Facebook.

With 19 years of experience in network marketing, social media and technology, I give to you what has worked for me as a distributor and tens of thousands of other distributors I worked with directly or indirectly throughout the years.

Brian Carter

I've been in Internet marketing since 1999. During that time, I've innovated in multiple areas: search engine optimization, pay-per-click advertising, email marketing, copywriting, conversion optimization, squeeze pages, lead gen, Facebook advertising, Twitter advertising, LinkedIn advertising and all types of social media. You may wonder if I'm a generalist. What I actually do is obsessively dive into a topic, read everything I can on it, find out what really works and what doesn't, do it for companies, further refine my sense of what works and what doesn't and then teach it. I am a results-focused system builder and teacher.

For example, in writing my book <u>LinkedIn For Business</u>, I discovered that although there are at least ten different LinkedIn marketing tactics, only three of them reliably create results. Because Internet marketing is so vast and complicated, and because every company has limited time and money, it's just as critical to know what's <u>not</u> worth doing as what you should do.

When Jim and I discussed this project, I had already written four books, been a professional speaker and taught Internet marketing to more than 10,000 people. We realized we would make a great team, and I was excited to see what Jim had discovered.

I've worked with and spoken to companies such as NBC, Microsoft and Marketo about digital marketing and social media. My agency has managed more than $1 million in Facebook ad budgets (and more than $2 million in Google ads), in addition to creating thousands of highly engaging daily social posts for a variety of companies. We've helped our clients get major results with Facebook, including fans, email leads, engagement and sales. I've seen clients get fans and post interactions for less than one cent each and ecommerce ROI's of up to 800 percent.

I've already written two social media books about Facebook, but this book is different. Jim is the network marketing expert, not me, and his success using Facebook for network marketing is the lynchpin of this book. I'm the backup on all types of Facebook marketing and what has worked for other companies that you can try out in network marketing.

Oh, and I'm the funny one. When I keynote speak, I'm all about practical takeaways, motivation and entertainment. When it comes to consulting, I'm drop-dead serious. It's all about getting you results.

So Read The Whole Book!

We hope you love this book and are confident that if you apply its lessons, you'll boost your income significantly!

Remember: If you want more than what's in the book... Bring the book to life with diagrams and how-to videos. Stay current with the latest changes in social media and how it can grow your business by joining our community: http://socialmediadirectsales.com/training

Want personal, one-on-one coaching? Go here: http://socialmediadirectsales.com/coaching

2. Facebook Is Part Of Your Strategy, Not The Whole Strategy

Most people try to rely on Facebook alone as their entire strategy when they are amateurs in our industry. They are looking for a fast way to make big money with little to no effort. They are looking for the magic bullet, the white elephant, the new shiny toy that takes them down the easy street to riches, and some "gurus" are happy to oblige. Just ten years ago, emailing someone a presentation was the magic bullet to riches, and seven years before that it was VHS tapes. We all want instant results. It is the reason fast food restaurants and instant oatmeal are so popular.

Frustration sets in when Facebook doesn't perform to their expectations. Is Facebook the problem? Not even close.

When you use Facebook as the lone strategy, it will fail you. When you use it as part of a bigger strategy, you will develop deep, meaningful relationships with those who eventually become customers and distributors on your team.

The whole strategy is comprised of passion, people skills and communication skills. This is what separates the amateurs from the pros. Facebook is part of the strategy, not the whole strategy.

You Need Passion

Why did you join your network marketing company? You can put every reason into two categories: you want to make more money or you want to have more time to do the things you love.

Want a new car, home or clothes for the family? That falls under "making more money." Want to see your children's basketball games or go on more family vacations rather than stay late at the office? These fall under "wanting more time in your life."

Understanding your passion keeps you going when times get tough. And they will. You are an entrepreneur now. You will also inspire everyone around you to chase their passion and never give up.

Think about it. Gini is ready to quit network marketing, so you give her a pep talk sharing your passion and why it means so much to have success in your network marketing company. She changes her mind and keeps pushing on. We understand because we've been there—several times!

You Need People Skills

People need to genuinely like you and vice versa. You're helping people by showing the value of your product and business. If they don't feel a connection with you, they'll find someone else to work with—even if they love your company.

For example, let's say Mike is taking a look at your business. You're excited, smiling and focusing on him while talking about all of the fun the both of you will have if he joins. Do you think he might become a distributor? There's a good chance.

You Need Communication Skills

You need to learn to get your point across with the least possible amount of words. Inspire others to become a customer and a distributor or refer you to someone else. You're excited. You believe you have the best product and opportunity in the world.

Once they're ready to join or buy, stop talking! If your friend is ready to be a customer, but you can't stop talking about every single feature, you may talk them out of taking action before you realize it.

Talk With People Face To Face

No matter how many friends you have on Facebook, nothing deepens a relationship like being with them in person. In person, you're more likely to have meaningful conversations about life and business than you are online. Do you only talk to your best friend on Facebook? Or do you spend time with them face to face? Being with them in person creates shared experiences that last a lifetime.

Imagine one of your distributors, Amanda, just enrolled her fourth distributor in one month, and she lives 10 minutes from you. You congratulate her on Facebook so that everyone else can join in cheering her on. Now think about how much more excited Amanda will be when you invite her out to a celebration lunch, as well.

Talk With People Over The Phone

As you build a team around the world, you can't meet with everyone face to face. The next best thing is a phone call. Did you know that your voice is as unique as your fingerprint? When we hear others' voices, we strengthen our relationships.

Steve, your newest distributor across the country, sends out 15 samples to friends and family in his first week. As always, you congratulate him on Facebook. Then you take that extra step and call him. He hears the excitement in your voice, and it motivates him to push beyond his comfort level. Steve hears, "You're doing a great job! I believe in you." No one ever believed in him before you. Do you think he's going to work even harder now? Yes.

Attend Company Events

You might think you can stay online and never attend a company event, but you'd be mistaken. Those who attend company events develop a different type of appreciation for the product and opportunity. They're the most passionate distributors in the company because they hear the vision directly from the company owners and executive team. They spend quality time with other distributors from around the world who also attend. A culture is shared at events and attendees take that back to pass on to their teams.

Sherry is on the fence about becoming a distributor with your company. She decides to attend an event with you. She meets 10 more people who are as excited as you are, all sharing customer testimonials. Sherry gets excited and comes on board the next morning.

Hand Out Samples (If Applicable)

Successful network marketing companies are customer-centric. They prioritize acquiring customers, not recruiting distributors. The products deliver such high value that each distributor will typically have 10 or 20 personal customers. Companies end up recruiting a lot of distributors indirectly in the process. Your team's best distributors start as the most passionate customers. They have an unwavering commitment to building the company long-term without jumping from one network marketing company to another. Instead of talking about how much money you can earn by being a distributor, first try handing out samples to capture interest for your products from your friends.

Pursue Personal Development

We all need to grow. We can all be better. We can't earn a six-figure income in network marketing without expanding our mind first. If you made $50,000 a year for the last 20 years, don't you think you need to change things about you in order to make $120,000? You do, and that change is between your ears. Most believe personal growth is the number one ingredient for success. We agree. Personal development happens by listening to audios, reading, attending events and having a personal coach.

Network Marketing Is A Numbers Game

It's easy to become frustrated when the people you know decide not to purchase your product or become a distributor. Rejection is the top reason people struggle with sales. You can ease your frustration by understanding the numbers of network marketing. On average, you will enroll one new distributor for every twenty people who look at your opportunity. For customers, it might be one out of every five who try a sample. Ask your company leadership to break down the numbers for your company. Understanding the numbers allows you to create a clear plan to success. Just because someone says no today doesn't mean they'll say no tomorrow. It's a timing issue.

At some point in a friend's life, they might need your product or business. It's your job to stay in touch with them as a friend until the timing is right.

Final Thoughts

Making Facebook part of your strategy means you'll never run out of conversation partners or opportunities to build strong relationships with current customers, distributors and friends who could be the next to join. And now that you understand how network marketing requires passion, people skills and communication skills, you'll be able to grow in them and apply them to Facebook without relying on Facebook alone.

NETWORK MARKETING FOR FACEBOOK

3. Why You Should Use Facebook

As a network marketing professional, success happens when someone buys your products then shares the results with her friends, motivating them to buy the product, too. This process repeats over and over, making you more money each time.

The more you share your products with others, the greater your success will be.

Since people sharing your products is one of the most important aspects of your business, wouldn't it make sense to join the community with the most people and the easiest ways for you to connect with them?

The best and largest community for networking and sales is Facebook. It has more than one billion users and is five times more popular than the next most popular social network.

The Future Of Network Marketing Is Now

In 2003, we were told by one of the most successful network marketing distributors of all time the following:

"If someone could figure out how to build

18

relationships on the Internet, they would build the biggest team of distributors in the history of network marketing."

Relationships with your friends, customers and distributors is the key to long-term success in our industry. Why? People order products and build business with those they know, like and trust. These three ingredients create the essence of a healthy relationship between you and another person. Think about your own network marketing business. Your best customers and distributors are those with whom you have the best relationships. Look at the most successful distributors in your company, as well. The same holds true for them.

The Internet has fascinated every network marketing professional since the mid-90s. The fastest way for us to build relationships pre-Internet was to invite friends to a weekly hotel or house meeting. Between these meetings, we shared cassette and VHS tapes that demonstrated the power of our products and the opportunity those products presented. Most friends didn't join until the meeting, which meant that it could take up to six days before they joined as a distributor. In the late 90's and early 2000's, we skipped the cassette and VHS tape step and emailed contacts a slide and, eventually, a video presentation. Friends signed up as customers and distributors in as little as a few hours. People were making buying and joining decisions much more quickly.

It wasn't until social networks (social media) that we had an Internet platform that could combine relationships with speed. As Facebook became the dominant player in the social media space and, undoubtedly, the easiest place online to build relationships, we got goose bumps. An eleven-year-old prediction from one of the most highly recognized distributors in network marketing had come true.

Facts About Facebook

Let's look at the facts about Facebook. As of June, 2014, Facebook boasted the following numbers:

1.32 billion people use Facebook every month on their computer.

1.07 billion people use Facebook every month on their mobile device, including cell phones, iPads and other tablets.

Do you know any other website that has this many active members in their community? There isn't one. Alexa currently has Facebook ranked at number two, right behind Google. Of course, Google is not really a community. Google Plus, Google's half-hearted attempt at social media, has had nowhere near the success of Twitter or Facebook.

Facebook has 7,185 employees, 14 offices in the United States and 34 international offices. This strong infrastructure allows Facebook to continue building features into a website that empowers network marketing professionals to thrive with their business.

The founder of Facebook, Mark Zuckerberg, said, "I want to connect the world." He isn't driven by money. His passion to connect people is your opportunity to build a successful network marketing business in a shorter period of time than was possible before social media.

There are other social media sites as well, but Facebook makes it easier than any of them to build relationships. Twitter's conversations are more fragmented and not gathered in any one place. On LinkedIn, in the few places where people gather often enough to converse, people are speaking from behind their professional personas, which can create walls rather than bridges. Facebook is better for conversations because people spend the most time there, you see comments for a post all together, and private messages are grouped in an even more convenient way than most email discussions. Seeing the conversation all together on Facebook makes meaningful interactions easier.

Let's check out Facebook's current features and how each benefits someone in network marketing.

Profile: People do business with you because they know, like and trust you. Your profile allows others to learn about you in the way you want. You can share your interests, photos, work history and more. Others can even see a timeline of your life on Facebook.

Newsfeed: People do business with you because you interact with them as a friend and not just about business. The Newsfeed is where you see posts from friends and pages you've liked. It shows you what your friends are posting on Facebook and allows you to interact with those posts. The Newsfeed is different for everyone. It's your personalized view of your Facebook community.

Graph Search: You never want to run out of people to speak with about your products. If you keep finding new people, eventually you'll gather enough customers to create your success. Graph Search makes it easy to connect with new people through the use of search phrases. For example: "Friends of friends who grew up in (your hometown)." When you reach out to these people, there is a mutual connection, making it more likely that they want to become friends and try your products.

Messenger: This is private messaging. Network marketing is about building relationships. The stronger your relationships, the more customers and distributors you have on your team. The fastest way to build a relationship is connecting with someone one on one. With

Messenger, you can send private messages (similar to email), make free phone calls all around the world, video chat (have face-to-face conversations without leaving the comfort of your home), text chat, and speak with many people privately at the same time.

Photos and Video: People often buy products for emotional reasons. First, they might hear an amazing testimonial from someone they trust. Then, they see their friends using your product. Next, they see a beautiful picture of the raw ingredients and read how impactful they can be to their lives. Photos and video capture the emotion of your product. Share that on Facebook by uploading an unlimited number of videos and high-resolution photos. You can create a story of your business through photo albums. You can even tag others. Tagging attaches the emotional power of friendships to each photo and video and can lead others to share it with their friends.

Pages: Your friends may know, like and trust you already. Guiding them to interact directly with the larger direct sales company allows you to focus on the relationship and not be the end-all-be-all expert on your product or opportunity. Pages gives the direct sales company a presence on Facebook. Once your friend likes your company's page, they will start to receive updates from the company. They can also share the company updates with their friends. Your company is working for you.

Groups: Your friends will become distributors on your team faster if they experience what it will be like before they join the company. Your existing team will be more successful if they have strong support available to them 24/7. Groups create a private space on Facebook where you communicate with your team and prospects. Groups connect you with other people who may have an interest in your products.

Events: As impressive as Facebook is for your business, you still need to meet with people face to face to build that unbreakable relationship for long-term business success. You can use Events to invite your friends to local, regional and national meetings for your company. Your friends can also invite others to the event, as well.

Gifts: Showing appreciation to one of your hard working distributors inspires them to build a bigger business. Gifts provide an easy way for you to send them a gift card from 150 different brands, such as Starbucks, Target and The Cheesecake Factory. You can even make the gesture public so others can see your gift.

Save: Success in network marketing requires growth in personal development and education in areas of your product, network marketing, people and communication skills. Create a library of saved materials to help you grow in each of these areas.

Facebook For Every Phone: You may have an interest in building your business in other countries. Those people need access to Facebook. Facebook For Every Phone is a partnership between Facebook and mobile operators, allowing more people to connect to Facebook in underserved countries.

Final Thoughts

If you're like us, your mind is probably swirling with the possibilities of how Facebook can help you achieve your success in network marketing.

If these features excite you, wait until you learn about the dozens of smaller features found throughout Facebook, such as friend and interest lists and happy birthday. We cover those in later chapters!

With over a billion people on Facebook, you can easily

find those who will love your products. Since three of every four smartphones have Facebook and more than half of users visit every day, it takes no effort to find people while they're "on the go."

You might find that your friends, family and those you met in the past are already on Facebook and would love to connect with you. How many of them might be interested in your products? Those who are not may refer your products to their friends if you share your products with them in a professional manner without hype. How many of their friends might be interested, as well? You can receive an endless supply of referrals if you run a professional business on Facebook.

Facebook gives you the opportunity to build real relationships with others. Think about it. Is a friend or a stranger more inclined to try your products and share them with friends? From our experience, friends are always more open to trying products and referring them to their friends.

Facebook is social proof. According to Robert Cialdini, who coined the term in his book <u>Influence</u>, social proof is when people copy what others are doing- they mimic and conform to others in an effort to behave correctly in any given situation. For example, if several people look at the sky, you may look up, too. If 20 people line up outside a restaurant, you'll tend to think it's a great restaurant and want to go in yourself. In Facebook, when your friends see you and others talking about a product over a certain period of time in their Newsfeed, they start to believe the product is good and they should at least try it.

Whether you are looking to build your business in your own backyard or share it around the world, Facebook is the perfect destination, a destination that allows you to meet unlimited amounts of people and build impeccable relationships with them—if you are willing to put in the time and effort. As you have probably heard many times in network marketing, relationships are the key to your success.

Remember: If you need more than the book...
Bring the book to life with diagrams and how-to videos. Stay current with the latest changes in social media and how it can grow your business by joining our community: http://socialmediadirectsales.com/training

Want personal, one-on-one coaching? Go here: http://socialmediadirectsales.com/coaching

4. Groups: Support Is Just A Few Clicks Away

We can move mountains when we belong to a group of passionate people working toward the same goals, supporting each other every day.

Support is a part of the foundation to success, and it works like this in network marketing:

Are you excited? Share this feeling with everyone so they can catch your excitement like a viral video.

Are you discouraged? Share this feeling with everyone so they can lift you up.

Do you have questions? Share them with everyone so they can answer them for you.

Whatever's on your mind, you can share it with a support team and never have to go through anything alone.

Imagine if you had access to a support team 24 hours a day. Your chances of failing virtually disappear.

A personal story from Jim:

In 2004, we met Nikki, a driven and passionate woman. She was contacting 10 to 15 new people a day about her network marketing business. She wanted to be the top recruiter in the company within 90 days. It was an impressive goal, but she needed to increase her numbers by 5 to 10 a day to achieve it. She was convinced she could not increase her numbers because of her hectic life: working a 9 to 5 job, rushing home to let the dogs out, cooking dinner while her children hung on her legs. How could she still find time to grow her business and spend time with her loving spouse? Like most people getting started in network marketing, she wasn't using her time effectively.

The support tool I used at the time was Yahoo Chat Messenger. If you were not on the Internet in 2004, the messenger worked the way Facebook Chat does today. Every night, we called the people who had requested more information about our business while supporting each other on Yahoo Chat.

The conversation on Yahoo Chat went as follows:

Jim: Oh boy! I am off to a rocking start! Six voicemails in a row. How are you doing?

Nikki: (laughs) I already got three people who are not interested.

Jim: Yes! Our first no! Isn't it fun talking to each other on chat while we are calling people who requested information about our business?

Nikki: It definitely makes calling people more fun, and I don't feel alone. Ah, shoot! This girl sounded promising. She wants to wait until next month, though. I am at four no's.

Jim: Boom! Just got a yes. I think this guy will do really great. He has been searching for an opportunity because he was just downsized.

Nikki: Wow! I got a yes! She wants to sign up right now. She already looked at the website.

Jim: Right on!

We had a blast. After 45 days, Nikki was the top recruiter in the company. She had achieved her goal.

Before Facebook Groups, a network marketing professional could only support a limited amount of people due to the technology available and ease of use.

But before we go into groups, let's explain why they work better for our purposes than Facebook Messenger or a Facebook Page.

Why Facebook Messenger and Facebook Pages Aren't Good Enough

Facebook Private Messages can't scale with your success.

Let's imagine a scenario. John creates a group and has 10,000 people on his network marketing team. He wants to invite all 10,000 to the group. Each of them invite three friends, and then we have 30,000 people in the group.

Messages require you to type in each person's name at some point, and this is just an unrealistic amount of work when you suddenly add hundreds or thousands of people.

When you create a Facebook Page and get fans, you can reach them by posting on your page, but not because they go back to your page. In fact, only about one percent of fans go back per month. The reason they see your post is that Facebook puts it in their Newsfeed. Remember, Newsfeed is the stream of posts you see when you log into Facebook or click on Home.

But Facebook doesn't show your page post to every fan. In fact, in 2013, Facebook admitted that the average page's posts only showed to about 16 percent of their fans. The well-known ad agency Ogilvy & Mather's research found a number closer to 6 percent.

Facebook does show posts they think people will like, so the pages that better understand their audience can reach more. Agorapulse, a Facebook tool company, found in May 2014 that famous athletes were still reaching an average of 33 percent of their fans. That means the most effective pages get more of their posts seen, but the ineffective page posts rarely reach anyone.

You want to reach as close to 100 percent as possible of the distributors you're supporting. Sixteen percent just isn't good enough.

The good news is that when you post or comment in a Group, everyone is notified (it shows up in that world icon that tells you there's new stuff). And if you've been on Facebook for any length of time, you know that notifications are addictive. When that globe gets a red number on it, you just have to see what's going on. So with a Group, you can reach a lot more of your people, a lot more of the time. That's how Facebook Groups can be more effective than Facebook Business Pages.

What is a Facebook Group?

More than 500 million people use Facebook Groups, a set of private online communities.

In 2010, a new, more engaging version of Facebook's Groups created the opportunity for network marketing professionals to support each other like never before—people easily connecting to each other in a private section on Facebook.

You can set up a Facebook Group for your network marketing team to communicate with each other, and you can make it private so that only they can access it. Within the group, your team can:

* Ask questions
* Seek advice
* Share product testimonials and success tips
* Organize events
* Share training materials
* Deepen team friendships

Groups also have a chat feature and group email address. Chat allows you to talk to someone when they are also on Facebook. Members of the group can send an email to the email address, and it will post in the group.

Besides supporting your team, consider inviting friends who show interest in your business into the group. Many will be instantly motivated to take action by seeing others excited about the business. As we always say, "Teamwork makes the dream work!" When they see your group's enthusiasm and togetherness, people become more interested in joining.

Let us share a personal story on how Facebook Groups inspired a friend to become a distributor.

In December of 2012, we met James on Facebook. He was an energetic family man from California. He expressed an interest in sharing our products with friends, so we invited him into our Facebook Group. In the first 30 days, we frequently saw James in the group commenting on other people's posts and posting questions. By the end of the first month, he enrolled as a distributor.

James enrolled because he witnessed first-hand the support he would receive if he chose to become a distributor.

How Facebook Groups Create Social Proof—And Sales!

Many people create a group too early in their network marketing career and it fails. When you are new in network marketing, you haven't yet developed the skills and experience to inspire and move large groups of people to action. When inspiration and action don't happen in the group, you end up creating confusion, doubt and the potential to lead people astray. We suggest you start your own group once you're earning a full-time income from network marketing. Until you achieve that, participate in a Facebook Group started by someone else above you who has already achieved that level of success. You'll learn more, succeed faster, and when you finally create your own group, it will have a much stronger impact.

A network marketing professional who is earning a full-time income can create social proof—one of the most motivating phenomena in social media—in a Facebook Group much easier than someone who is only earning a part-time income.

Social proof is one reason Facebook Groups contribute so powerfully to success.

Let us explain with two group experiences, one good, and the other bad:

Group One: We sample your product, and we're interested in sharing it with our friends. You add us to your group so we can see what it would be like working together with everyone. While in the group, we notice there are 100 other members. But no one is talking to each other. Interaction is low. In fact, nobody even welcomes us into the group!

Group Two: We sample your product, and we're interested in sharing it with our friends. You add us to your group so we can see what it would be like working together with everyone. While in the group, we notice there are 500 other members, and everyone is talking to each other. Interaction is high. Over 20 people welcome us to the group and share why they love the product. Wow!

Which of those two groups would you rather join? Group two. It's a no-brainer.

Group Two demonstrates social proof. Those earning a full-time income can usually build a bigger group quickly by inviting their existing team into it.

Generating sales using social proof allows you to leverage the excitement of others when talking to people about your products. You never have to high pressure sell someone again. The evidence created by the social proof makes it easier for you to sell, and in some cases, social proof sells both the products and the opportunity without your help.

How Members Can Get The Most Out Of Facebook Groups

As a member of the group, check in several times a week. Sometimes it makes sense to check in every day.

Always like and comment on what other members are posting in the group. Some people like every comment posted in the group. This means you're not playing favorites, and you're creating good will with everyone. Only comment when you have something meaningful to share with the group.

Post something in the group at least a few times a week. It could be a question, words of motivation, pictures or videos. Be creative. The goal is to be <u>social</u>.

How Admins Can Get The Most Out Of Facebook Groups

If you're an admin for the group, check into the group

a few times a day. It is your responsibility to lead the group.

Interact with others the same way members do.

Post something in the group every day. You are at the top position in your company. Others are looking at you for guidance. It is your responsibility to support your entire team with words of inspiration and answer questions for those who are prospects in the group.

Members won't know if you're an admin unless you tell them. If you are an admin, you are a leader, and should act like one.

All posts should be check marked to ensure you are notified every time someone posts, likes and comments in the group.

Pin a message at the top of your group.

For example you can say,

WATCH VIDEO BELOW!

See why thousands of people are talking about (your company).

Why join the (name) Facebook Group? So, you will never be alone! Whether it is support, advice or encouragement, you can work closely with others and those at corporate. Invite your fellow distributors and friends who are curious about being one.

We are looking forward to seeing your success with our company!

Tips When Setting Up The Group

Be sure the name of the group is in compliance with your company. You can make the group one of several different levels of privacy. Here are the three levels:

Open: Anyone can see the group, who's in it and what

members post.

Closed: Anyone can see the group and who's in it. Only members see posts.

Secret: Only members see the group, who's in it and what members post.

It's up to you which group privacy you choose based on how you want to lead your team. Personally, we like open because it allows us to show prospects the experience of working with us before they join as a distributor. Also, if you have an open group, your team can share its posts easily with their friends on Facebook. That's not the case with a closed group. Closed group posts can't be shared with non-members.

Here are a few more elements of Facebook Groups:

Membership Approval: We like to set groups so that any member can add members, but an admin must approve them. This practice allows you to decide who can and can't join the group.

Description: Write a short paragraph that explains your opportunity. Potential members see the description if privacy is set to open or closed. The description is a good place to put a few sentences on group policy. What is allowed and what isn't? Later if you see any behavior you don't like, modify this description to address that.

Tags: Tags help people find groups about certain topics. This can help generate new leads for you and your team. We suggest words related to your product and business.

Posting Permissions: We recommend "members and admins can post to the group." The goal is to build community and culture.

Post Approval: We prefer "all group posts must be

approved by an admin." This protects you from someone spamming your group.

Events: Create events for local, regional and national gatherings. Events allows your team to easily share with all their friends on Facebook. You will notice more people show up at your events when utilizing this feature on Facebook.

Files: Every leader has unique training based on their life experiences. Create a new document or upload a file to share your training with your team.

When And How To Add Friends To A Facebook Group

Very important: only add your friends to the group if they are interested in sharing your products with their friends as a distributor. If they are only interested in purchasing your products as a customer, they will visit the company's Facebook page only. Add them yourself or provide the Facebook Group link and they can join themselves. Most people consider it rude if you add them to a group without their approval. You might even lose them as a friend. Be respectful.

When adding your friends, welcome them to the group by saying, "Hey, everyone! I would like you to meet my friend, Marianne. She tried a sample and is excited to learn more about the business. She is looking to make extra income." This simple gesture will make your friend feel welcomed. When you see someone else in the group add a friend, welcome them by leaving a comment. For example, "Hi Marianne! Welcome to the group! I joined this business because the product helped me personally. I also wanted to earn a part-time income from home. So far, I have three customers!" This simple gesture will not only make the new person feel welcomed, it motivates others to welcome your friends when you add them in the group. You're training them how to act in the group, leading by example.

Final Thoughts

Why does everyone in network marketing promote the next event? Every leader in our industry understands that when a person comes to a live event, their chances of success increase exponentially. People leave events inspired, motivated and confident.

A Facebook Group is a live event happening 24 hours a day. When run correctly, it will become the cornerstone of your Facebook success. We challenge you to create a group that is run this way. Give inspiration to your team and motivate your distributor-prospects to join the team. You have something that could change their life.

5. What Does Your Facebook Profile Say About You?

When someone knows, likes and trusts you, they are more willing to sample your product, become a customer and even share the product with their friends.

Your Facebook profile gives you the opportunity to leverage that "know-like-trust" idea on Facebook by using your profile picture, cover image and "about" section properly.

Knowing, liking and trusting happens in three steps:

1. Getting to know you
2. Beginning to like you
3. Beginning to trust you

Keep in mind, your profile is a way to organize your life and tell your story on Facebook. As you explore the Facebook community and meet others, your profile becomes your home. When others want to learn more about you, they visit your profile.

Step 1: Getting to Know You

People will come to know you by your profile picture (sometimes called an avatar). Each time you like or comment on a post anywhere on Facebook, your profile picture will be seen by others. It is your primary identity on Facebook.

Here are two tips to ensure you have a successful profile picture:

1. People can't get to know you if they can't see you. Make the most of this small space. Choose a close-up with a bright smile.

2. We don't recommend a picture with your pet or a family member. People aren't going to do business with Fido or your cousin. They are going to do business with you. Also, if you have a spouse or girlfriend in your photo, depending on your first name, they may not know which one is you!

Once you find the picture that works for you, we recommend you stick with it. People are busy, and they scroll through their Newsfeed quickly when reading what friends are posting. By staying consistent with your picture, they will recognize it quickly, and you have a better chance of them reading your post. It's the same reason why companies like Starbucks and Pepsi don't change their logo all the time. If they did, we wouldn't recognize their ads, and their advertising and marketing dollars would be wasted. Don't waste the chances you have to make an impact on Facebook.

To add a profile picture, choose an image from your Facebook Photo Albums, take a photo using your computer camera or upload a photo from your computer or phone. Once you select your picture, make sure it's centered.

Don't forget: big smile!

Step 2: Beginning to Like You

People will come to like you by your cover image. When someone visits your profile, the cover image will be the first thing they see. It gives them a snapshot of your life and personality.

Here are two tips to ensure you select a successful cover picture:

1. This is a much bigger space than your profile picture. Not only do we recommend a picture of you, we also suggest family pictures or an event in your life. Events can range from a picture of you spending time with your family to standing on stage receiving an award for your network marketing accomplishments. The goal is to show your personality through a picture.

2. It is possible to post a picture that turns people off. We recommend staying neutral on topics that are controversial and polarizing. For example, we wouldn't post a picture of you supporting or opposing specific politicians. You may choose to disagree, but be ready to lose customers who don't agree with you. In these polarizing times, be ready to lose half your potential customers in order to express your views.

We recommend you constantly change your cover picture to keep it current with what's going on in your life. You're always growing and becoming a better person, so let people see your growth and accomplishments through your cover image. Every time you update it, friends have a chance to like and comment on it, so it's another opportunity to build relationships.

Step 3: Beginning to Trust You

People will come to trust you through your "About" section. In this section, share your work history, education, where you went to high school and college, where you are currently living and have lived, contact information, basic information, relationship status, family members, your photos, your friends, favorite books and music, movies and TV shows, and even which Facebook pages you have liked.

Tips For A Successful "About" Section:

Share your work history dating back to your very first job, even if it was 50 years ago. A thorough history of your career connects you to others who worked, and still work, in the same companies. It shows potential customers that you're a real person. Don't be ashamed if your career is not incredible. The goal is to be honest and transparent, not show that you were the VP of Marketing for a large company. Sometimes people connect more to people who came from less stellar origins or who are at the same experience level.

Share your education. It will connect you to others who went to or are still attending your same high school or university. Education opens you up to hundreds of thousands of potential customers for your product. A school in common is often enough to create trust with an otherwise complete stranger.

Share where you're living, have lived and grew up to connect to people from those areas. When reaching out to new people on Facebook, common ground is powerful.

Share your contact information. You don't have to fill out everything in this section. You may not be comfortable showing your phone number. However, filling out this information is like handing someone a business card. It gives them the ability to reach out to you. It also builds trust, because open, confident people seem more trustworthy than anonymous, private ones.

Share your basic information. It will help develop deeper relationships. They'll be able to wish you a happy birthday and vice versa. There's nothing quite like getting 100 happy birthday messages through Facebook. It means a lot to some people when you wish them well. And on that note, write something original for each person and send it to them as a private message. Yours will stand out and mean more to them.

Share what type of relationship you're in and with whom. This expands your friends through your partner— more potential new customers. For example, your husband likes one of your posts. His friend's spouse comments on the post as well. She notices you are her husband's friend's spouse. Trust immediately rises, and she is more open to trying a sample.

Share your family members. It creates the same opportunity as when you shared your relationship. You can add all of your family members or the ones closest to you.

Regularly post pictures on Facebook, weekly or daily, so that they appear in your "About" section. The most engaging kind of Facebook content is pictures. People love looking at them and commenting on them. Photos tell a story, and it's easy to interact with them. When someone has 20 minutes before their lunch break is over, they may skim Facebook to see what their friends are doing. They're checking quickly, so pictures catch their eye faster than plain text.

Keep increasing the amount of friends you have on Facebook. While scrolling through your "About" section, do you think people will be more impressed if you have 50 or 1,000 friends? They'll think you're more active on Facebook if you have more friends. But don't add friends just to grow your numbers. Choose people you would want to be friends with in the real world. Trusted friendships are always the first ones to sample your products. If you add too many people you don't know, they may complain and Facebook might put you on friend-adding timeout for a while.

Share your favorite books, music, movies and TV shows. Connect with others who have similar interests. Remember, having common ground with someone increases trust, and they are more willing to try a sample of your product. Trust will increase with your existing friends because they'll know a little bit more about you.

Share your Facebook Check-ins. Bond with others who have traveled to the same places. Share experiences. Isn't commonality what makes great friendships? Of course! Great friends try your products and eventually become distributors.

Share the Facebook pages you've liked. You can connect with others who have liked the same pages.

Here are two scenarios of what can happen when you fill out your profile successfully and unsuccessfully:

You meet Tracy on Facebook and decide you want to stay in touch with her. You send her a friend request. She is notified of your intention. Instead of just accepting your friend request, she looks at your profile picture.

Scenario One: You Followed Our Profile Recommendations

She smiles back at your contagious smile in your profile picture. She clicks on it to visit your profile. She says,

"Aww…" because your cover image shows you, your son and your puppy playing in a green field. She likes you at this point, but she still checks out your "About" section.

Tracy wants to make sure you're a real person. She notices you and her husband worked at the same company the year she was married, so she starts to reminisce about her wedding day. She chuckles when she sees you went to the same university as her crazy cousin Amy.

She wonders if you know Uncle Teddy because you both grew up in the same hometown. She smiles when she sees your birthday is on the same day as her best friend. She finishes reading your "About" section and discovers that you have similar tastes in music and movies.

Scenario Two: You Didn't Implement Our Profile Recommendations

Your profile picture is hard to see because it is a full body shot of you. She decides to visit your profile anyway since you were kind enough to reach out to her.

Tracy gives a hmm…because your cover image is all about making money and getting rich. She knows there are a lot more important things in life than driving a Ferrari. She notices on your "About" section you listed just one job and it's vague.

She can't find where you went to high school or college. She sees your current city, but doesn't know where you lived or your hometown. She notices your contact and basic information is blank as well. You liked only two movies, but she's never heard of either one.

Final Thoughts

A real friendship between two people starts with understanding each other. Your best customers and distributors are those who know, like and trust you.

Remember: If you need more than the book...
Bring the book to life with diagrams and how-to videos.
Stay current with the latest changes in social media and
how it can grow your business by joining our community:
http://socialmediadirectsales.com/training

Want personal, one-on-one coaching? Go here:
http://socialmediadirectsales.com/coaching

6. Go Public On Facebook

It's time to introduce your products to all of your friends. The fastest way is to publish a post in your Newsfeed.

Three Easy Steps To Writing A Successful Post

<u>Step 1:</u> Introduce your post. Don't talk about the business or products. You are not a salesperson. You are a friend. This can be an informal, "Hey, everyone!"

<u>Step 2:</u> One personal and one product statement. Write only two sentences. Keep it simple. For example, "As you may know, I am cautious with what products I put on my body. I found a 100% natural, organic skincare line that I am using daily."

<u>Step 3:</u> Pose a question to continue the conversation. Make it easy on them by asking one question. This allows people to make a quick decision. Multiple questions can confuse them and make them decide it's easier to skip answering any of them. It can be as simple as, "Would you like a free sample?"

The following will ensure you create a successful post. We've studied the Facebook Insights for thousands of

Facebook pages. Usually, the greatest proportion of page fans were using Facebook between 8 p.m. and 9 p.m. in their time zone. Post at 8 p.m. in your time zone if it's a weekday. Post anytime on a weekend.

Talk to your friends in the same way you want to be spoken to. It will allow you to write posts in a way that is comforting to your friends. If they feel the high-pressure sale, they won't move forward as a customer, and you may even lose them as a friend.

Focus on sampling the product as opposed to asking them about the distributor opportunity. Typically, one out of five people will order your product after receiving a sample, but only one out of every 20 will become a distributor after you ask them if they want to make money. The math here says that talking about the sample is four times more effective than talking about money. And once you have a customer, you have someone who yet might also become a distributor.

According to the Direct Selling Association, all network marketing companies fall into one of six product categories. The following are examples of more and less effective posts for each category. (Always rephrase these in your own words.)

Home/Family Care

More Effective Post:

Hey everyone! As you may know, I am cautious with what products I use in my home. I found a 100% natural and safe home product line, ranging from cleaning products to clothing detergent.

Would you like a sample? (Put the question on its own line, so it catches your friend's attention. The question moves them closer to being a customer.)

Less Effective Post:

I found the most amazing business! You can get all your home products with no chemicals in them. Save your family from the cancer chemicals found in cleaning products! You got to check this out now. I will send you free samples, and you can make money, too, and get rich with me! (Even if this message is true, people have learned that if it sounds too good to be true, it most likely is and therefore should stay away from it.)

Wellness

More Effective:

Hey everyone! As you may know, I am cautious about the products I put in my body. I found a product line that I believe can help you live a healthy lifestyle, and I use it daily now.

Would you like a sample?

Less Effective:

I can't believe what I just found! My friend was cured from cancer just by using this product. I know this is hard to believe, please just trust me. I will send you a sample today. OMG!

Personal Care

More Effective:

Hey everyone! As you may know, I am cautious with what products I put on my body. I found a 100% natural, organic skincare line that I am using daily.

Would you like a sample?

Less Effective:

OMG! My friend is making $10,000 a month with these new radical skincare products that are making everyone's skin feel like a baby's butt. Anyone interested? I will send you samples. I think I just won the lottery!

Services & Others

More Effective:

Hey everyone! As you may know, I am always looking for ways to save money. I found a way to save money on my electricity bill.

Would you like for me to see if I can save you money on your electricity bill?

Less Effective:

Would you like to become rich by helping your friends save money on their electric bill? I saved 80% on my last month's bill! You will be nuts if you don't jump on board. Once in a lifetime opportunity!

Clothing & Accessories

More Effective:

Hey everyone! As you may know, I am always into finding the next beautiful piece of jewelry. I found an amazing new line.

Would you like to check it out?

Less Effective:

Girls! I just bought the most amazing jewelry and now I am a jewelry consultant. I get paid 40% commission for selling it on Facebook and having virtual home parties. Do you want to check out the jewelry and sell it with me?

Leisure & Educational

More Effective:

Hey everyone! As you may know, I love traveling. I found a company that saves me up to 50% off my trips.

Would you like to check it out for your next vacation?

Less Effective:

Travel the world for free! Yes, I said it! FREE... Send me a private message and ask me how!

Completing Your Post

Once you write your post, add a picture of you with your products. Be proud that you are launching your business. Smile! Smiles are contagious, and they drive people to ask for more information.

After your picture is uploaded, start tagging. Tagging is effective because it creates social proof within a post. When your friends see that you are working with others, it raises their curiosity to check out your products. Only tag those who introduced you, your sponsor, to the direct sales company. People only like to be tagged on Facebook if their face is in the picture. In network marketing, they also like to be tagged for financial reasons. Your sponsor becomes successful by helping you become successful. If your sponsor is tagged, it allows the sponsor to be notified by Facebook so the sponsor can comment on your post, creating social proof for you. It also creates a two-way street. Your sponsor's friends can also see the post, and it helps them to create social proof around the products within their friend network. Teamwork makes the dream work.

Here are two ways tagging is powerful:

You tag the person who introduced you to the business. Their friends now have the opportunity to see your post. It may generate a new customer for your friend.

The people who sign up as distributors because of you will now tag your name. Distributors will tag your name as long as they feel you are providing support to their business so they can be successful. Support can be as simple as reaching out to them weekly to see if they need anything. Your friends will have the opportunity to see their post. You may get a new customer out of it.

After you are done tagging, make the post emotional. Are you happy? Excited? Nervous? Choose your smiley face and expression.

Before posting, make sure it says, 'public' next to the post button. If not, only a select group of friends may see your post.

Final Thoughts

Going public on Facebook means you can introduce your products to all of your friends in a professional manner. This can create instant sales for you.

7. Go Personal On Facebook With Messages

How many friends do you currently have on Facebook? 50? 100? 1,000? Wouldn't it be great to send each one a private message to make sure they know about your products?

You can by using Facebook Messenger.

Facebook Messenger is just like email, and a growing number of people use them at least as much as email. They allow you to communicate privately or with a group of people.

Facebook Messenger is more organized than email. It archives your Facebook Chats so you can review a history of communication between you and a friend.

Imagine one year after you send your friend a sample, he wants to talk again about being a customer. You can review the last year of conversations before talking to him.

We recommend that you reach out to all of your existing friends before adding new ones. You already have a relationship with your existing friends, so they are more likely to become a customer than someone you just met. We've seen new distributors contact new people on

51

Facebook instead of reaching out to their existing friends first. Many times their existing friends purchased product or became a distributor with someone else. Don't let that happen to you. It's easier and smarter to talk to your friends first.

You never know who is looking for your type of product until you ask. Jim's friend, Chanelle, is a fitness model in Arizona. Many would never talk to her about a skincare line because she already has flawless skin. But she recently sampled an all-natural and organic skincare product line from a network marketing company and loved it so much that she became a customer. You never know who'll be interested in your product.

Before Messaging Your Friends

If you haven't spoken to your Facebook friend in a while, make sure to reestablish the relationship before you talk to them about your products. You don't want your friend to feel like you are only reaching out to them to earn money by selling your products.

For example you can say, "Hey! We haven't spoken in a while. How have you been?"

Only chat about your products if they ask what you are doing with yourself these days. They will learn about your products by seeing your posts in their Newsfeed if they don't ask.

How to Message

Use the same three step process from the last chapter, changing only the words in step 1. In step 1, we taught you to say, "Hey everyone!" but since you're one-on-one here, just say, "Hey! How are you?"

Personalize your messages based on what you know about your friend. For example, you may know he or she needs to make extra money or use your product for a specific, personal reason.

An 'Extra Money' Message

Hi Lisa! How are you? I remember talking with you in the past about making extra money. I found something. Should I send you more information?

A 'Use Your Product For A Specific Personal Reason' Message

Here are examples of personal messages for each of the six main MLM categories. Always rephrase these in your own words.

Home/Family Care

Hi! How are you? I remember talking with you in the past about how dangerous traditional cleaning products are in the home. I found a 100% natural and safe home product line, ranging from cleaning products to clothing detergent.

Would you like a sample?

Wellness

Hi! How are you? I remember talking with you in the past about how it would be nice to lose 20 pounds for the summer. I found a product line that I believe can help us.

Would you like a sample?

Personal Care

Hi! How are you? I remember talking with you in the past about how you don't like how your shampoo makes your hair feel. I found a 100% natural, organic skincare line for your hair.

Would you like a sample?

Services & Others

Hi! How are you? I remember talking with you in the past about how it would be nice to save some money. I found a way to save money on my electricity bill.

Would you like for me to see if I can save you money on your electricity bill?

Clothing & Accessories

Hi! How are you? I remember talking with you in the past about how you loved jewelry. I found an amazing new line.

Would you like to check it out?

Leisure & Educational

Hi! How are you? I remember talking with you in the past about how you love to travel. I found a company that saves me up to 50% off of my trips.

Would you like to check it out for your next vacation?

How To Make Hundreds of Messages More Manageable

A great goal when reaching out to your Facebook friends is to contact 10 of them per day. Over the course of a month, this equates to 300 new people learning about your products. It should only take you 10 minutes a day to achieve these numbers.

Even if you are an over-achiever, don't contact more than 10 new friends per day. Facebook monitors how quickly you contact your friends with similar messages. We have seen people send messages to 100 people in one day and been blocked from sending new messages for 30 days. That can slow the growth of your business.

What Kind of Results Should You Expect?

This is a numbers game. Some will say yes. Some will say no. Some won't even respond. It's okay. Not everyone will have an interest in your products.

Here's an example from Jim's wife to help you gain a deeper understanding of numbers.

Recently in Marianne's network marketing business, she sent out private messages to 792 Facebook friends.

Here's what happened:

672 people did not respond at all.
120 responded with a yes or no.
85 of them requested a sample.
35 were not interested.
17 became customers.

Most people at this point ask similar questions about the numbers. Let's go through these.

Why Did 672 People Ignore Her Message? That's A Lot!

There are a bunch of possible reasons:

They may not have seen her message yet.

They may be interested but left Facebook because their dinner was burning on the stove and they forgot to reply later.

They may not be interested, left Facebook because their son spilled milk on the new carpet and forgot to reply later.

They may not be interested, and they didn't feel the need to respond.

They may not be interested but didn't want her to feel bad and thought no response was more polite than replying with a "no."

Most likely, the majority didn't respond because she doesn't yet have a deep, meaningful relationship with them. Relationships take time to build, and most of these people will end up trying the product later as she posts quality content about her products on Facebook.

Should she be upset that 672 people didn't respond?

No. Marianne is a network marketing professional. She focuses on what she achieved, which was 17 new customers. Each of these 17 people have, on average, 200 Facebook friends. She just expanded her list of people who may want a sample by 3,400. If someone uses and likes your product, they are most likely willing to share it with their friends. Even if she acquired one new customer out of the 792, it still expanded her list of potential customers by 200.

Which numbers are important?

All of them. For those who do not respond, you need to build a stronger relationship. Pay special attention to their posts when liking and commenting on friend's posts. If you really like one of their posts, send them a private message to let them know. If someone says no to trying a sample, make sure you at least like their posts in your Newsfeed. This will increase the chances of them seeing your business posts. Life is about timing. One day, they may need your product. Make sure you are the one they think of during this time.

Out of 85 sample requesters, 17 became a customer. That's one out of five, or 20 percent. In Marianne's company, this percent is a companywide goal based on their own testing. It means she is putting them through the process correctly and doesn't need to tweak it.

Final Thoughts

You should have a numbers-driven mind-set. Understanding the numbers allows you to make educated decisions so you can create a successful business.

Remember: If you need more than the book...

Bring the book to life with diagrams and how-to videos. Stay current with the latest changes in social media and how it can grow your business by joining our community: http://socialmediadirectsales.com/training

Want personal, one-on-one coaching? Go here: http://socialmediadirectsales.com/coaching

8. How To Respond When Friends Message Back

It's exciting to have someone respond to your Facebook Message. Let's make sure they're really interested in your products by giving them some solid information.

This step is especially important for those who will be sending samples because it will save you time and money. It will give you a better conversion rate because you'll eliminate the people who aren't really interested. If you acquire one customer for every five samples (20 percent conversion rate), you may notice it improve to one out of every three (33 percent conversion rate, 65 percent better than that 20 percent conversion rate).

Writing a successful response takes three easy steps:

Step 1: Thank your friend for responding to your message.

Step 2: Give some information. The best types of information here are company marketing videos, customer testimonials and product details.

Step 3: Let them know the next step they should take.

Here's a message you can use, but feel free to personalize it:

Thanks for getting back to me! To make sure you like the products, check out our Facebook photo albums below. Let me know what you think, and I'll drop a sample in the mail. Also, what is your mailing address?

60+ Life Changing Stories: (Link to a customer testimonial photo album located on your company's Facebook Page.)

Breakdown Of Each Product: (Link to a product description photo album located on your company's Facebook Page.)

Thanks,

Your Name

Follow Up

Send this additional message once a week only if you don't hear back from your friend:

Hey! You mentioned you wanted to try out my products. Did you have a chance to check out our Facebook Page?

Let me know, and I'll drop a sample in the mail.

Can't wait to hear from you!

Thanks,

Your Name

People get busy and not everyone checks Facebook daily. Be patient. The last thing you want to do is send a sample to someone who isn't interested. Save your samples for those who respond to you. Keep sending a friendly message once a week, and they'll get back to you when they are ready.

As people are responding, how do you stay in touch with them on Facebook? You create lists. Lists are an easy way for you to organize your friends on Facebook based on their interest level with your products.

Organize your friends using the following lists:
1. Prospects
2. Samples
3. Customers
4. Team

When they respond about whether they want to try a sample, it'll either be a YES or NO. Their response determines what list they go to next.

Your Friend Said, "No" To A Sample

If handled properly, most will say yes in time.

Here is a message you can use. Try to personalize it:

"OK, no problem! Thanks for getting back to me. How have you been?"

Next, put them in a Facebook list called Prospects.

Prospects is compiled of people who responded to any of your messages but aren't interested in receiving a sample.

If your friend says no, focus on building a relationship, and they will try your products in the future.

Your Friend Said, "Yes" To A Sample

If handled properly, most will become a customer after they receive the sample.

Here is a message you can use. Feel free to personalize it:

Hey! I just sent out your sample. Let me know what you think after you try it.

Your Name

Next, put them in a Facebook list called Samples.

Samples is compiled of people who have been sent a sample.

Now it's time to ask for the sale. Remember, not all samples turn into customers. Here is a message you can use. Feel free to personalize it.

Hey! How are you enjoying the samples? Let me know if you have any questions.

I wanted to let you know about this month's product promotion. It is _____.

The website is (enter your website). Just click on _____ to see the promotion this month.

Looking forward to hearing from you!

Your Name

Your Friend Hasn't Responded To The Sample Offer

Until they become a customer or say no, you should send a friendly message once a week.

Here are messages you can use. Be sure to personalize them:

"Hey! I sent you a message last week. How are you enjoying the samples?"

OR

"Hey! Did you have a chance to place your order? I want to make sure you get your product on time."

OR

"Hey! Thanks for trying the samples. If you know

anyone who is into these type of products, please send them my way."

If your friend becomes a customer, move them from the Sample list to the Customer list.

Waiting For The "No's" To Be Ready

Do you notice most people don't become a customer the first time you speak with them? It isn't because of the product or business, rather the timing of where they are in their life. Your friend has to be ready to accept that your product or business can benefit them.

Here are examples in the six main direct sales categories:

Home/Family Care

Sarah says no to trying a sample from you. Three months later, her two-year-old daughter accidentally drinks clothing detergent and is rushed to the hospital. Thankfully her daughter is okay, but she now realizes how dangerous chemical-based home products can be to her family. The next day she sees a business post from you about how safe your home products are for your family.

It's a good bet the timing is right, and she's ready to try a sample now.

Wellness

Ben says no to trying a sample from you. One year later his doctor informs him that he will have a heart attack unless he loses 50 pounds. He now realizes to the importance of a healthy lifestyle. The next day he sees a business post from you about how much weight you lost over the past year because you stayed committed to the product.

Do you think your story may motivate him to try your

product?

Personal Care

Alicia says no to trying a sample from you. Two weeks later, she breaks out in a rash from one of her skincare products. She now realizes her current products might not be the best. The next day she sees a business post from you about how you helped another friend with your chemical-free skincare products.

Do you think your friend's testimonial may inspire her to reach out to you?

Services & Others

Georgio says no to saving money on his electricity bill. For the next six months he continues to pay over $300 a month on his bill. In the same timeframe, he consistently sees how much money you save on your own bill and how many other people you are helping because you share all the great news on Facebook. In the seventh month, he calls his electricity company to resolve a problem but only receives poor customer service.

Sometimes frustrations lead people to seek other alternatives. He may be ready to chat with you.

Clothing & Accessories

Mary says no to checking out your jewelry. Two days later her best friend invites her to a party. She realizes she doesn't have a piece of jewelry to match her new dress. Later that day, she sees your business post showcasing a piece of jewelry that would go great with her dress.

It's only a matter of time until a woman needs a great piece of jewelry for an event, so why not be the person ready and willing to help?

Leisure & Educational

Joe says no to checking out all the great travel deals from your company. Five years later, he travels to Greece and realizes he could have saved $2,000. Upon his return, he saw a business post from you where it showed a Greece getaway for half the price.

Sometimes it takes losing money to finally look for ways to save it. Will you be there to help them when they are ready?

Sometimes "no" means "not now," and your prospect doesn't realize she is going to change her mind a week or a month later. This timing issue isn't unique to your company or direct sales. Every business, everywhere, has the same experience.

Final Thoughts

You will acquire more customers and save money on samples when you have your friends review information before sending them a sample. It opens their eyes to why they should be using your product long-term.

The conversation happening between the first time they reach out to you and the decision to become a customer should be laid back and low pressure.

You are looking to help them live a better life with your product, not trying to make a fast commission. The result will be someone who uses your product for many years and refers it to friends.

9. How To Turn Customers Into Distributors

If you love a product, it's only natural you'll share it with your friends and family. Reward your customers financially when they share your products.

Contact your customers two weeks after they been on the products.

Here is a message you can use. Don't forget to personalize it:

Hey! How are you enjoying the products?

Would you have an interest sharing these products on Facebook for some extra income? It, literally, takes 20 minutes a day.

We have a Facebook Group where you can learn more and meet people who are earning a part-time and full-time income.

Here is the link: (insert link here)

What do you think?

Your Name

If your friend becomes a distributor, move them from the Customer to the Team list.

At this point, be sure to re-read chapter three to review how to use the Facebook Group to inspire your friends to become a distributor for your company.

Final Thoughts

The most successful distributors on your team are those who have a personal product testimonial or know someone who has been positively impacted by your products. The more successful distributors that are on your team, the bigger your financial success. Doesn't it make sense to ask your customers if they have an interest in sharing a product they love with their friends?

Remember: If you need more than the book...
Bring the book to life with diagrams and how-to videos. Stay current with the latest changes in social media and how it can grow your business by joining our community: http://socialmediadirectsales.com/training

Want personal, one-on-one coaching? Go here: http://socialmediadirectsales.com/coaching

10. Why It's Critical To Stay In Touch With Friends

Distributors who succeed are those who stay in touch with friends until they're ready to take a look. It's only a matter of time until friends try a sample. Facebook makes it easy to stay in touch with your friends.

There are two ways of staying in touch on Facebook:

1. Posting quality content

2. Interacting with your friends' posts.

Posting quality content is an art. It is the balance between business and personal. Too much of either can result in failure. Balance it properly, and you may end up the most successful distributor in your company.

Balancing Personal And Business

Post about personal stuff 80 percent of the time. People do business with those whom they have the best relationship, so let your friends see your real life. Post about life events and what's on your mind.

Post about business matters 20 percent of the time.

How do you talk to your friends in person or over the phone? Turn that conversation into a Facebook post and include a picture or video to bring your words to life.

If you are on Facebook once a day, here is how a week's worth of effective Facebook posts may look:

<u>Monday:</u> I ran three miles today. I love shedding weight and being in shape!

<u>Tuesday:</u> Jade and I are going shopping today. She loves the sneaker store!

<u>Wednesday:</u> It's really nice earning a part-time income working from home. Now, I need to figure out where to spend this extra $300 dollars. Any thoughts?

<u>Thursday:</u> Hubby and I went out to dinner tonight at this amazing restaurant. I love when he surprises me!

<u>Friday:</u> Little Joey is so adorable when he plays in his basketball games. I love seeing him grow up.

<u>Saturday:</u> Fun in the sun! Glad I am protected with my natural & organic skincare. Let me know if you want a sample.

<u>Sunday:</u> Great sermon today! It really touched my heart.

See how only two of the seven posts above are about business?

The 80/20 Rule And How It Applies Based On How Much You Post A Day

1. If you post once a day, that's seven posts a week. Five should be personal and two about business.

2. If you post twice a day, that's 14 posts a week. Eleven should be personal and three about business.

3. If you post three times a day, that's 21 posts a week.

Sixteen should be personal and five about business.

Posting more about business does not help you get more customers. It only turns off your friends.

Sharing And Adding To Company Posts

Instead of trying to come up with your own clever business posts, try sharing posts from your direct sales company's Facebook page. Scroll through their page and click 'share' when you find a post you like or click on photos and choose from one of the albums.

It's important to write a few personal sentences along with your company's post. Making it personal is why it works.

Here are examples of a few personal sentences you could add to the company post based on the six product categories in Direct Sales. Always rephrase these in your own words.

Home/Family Care

I used this carpet cleaning product last Tuesday, and it got out all the stains left by my lovely dog. Check it out below!

(company post will appear here)

Wellness

I already lost 10 lbs. on this product. Check out the testimonial below. This girl lost 75 lbs. over the last year! Very impressive!

(company post will appear here)

Personal Care

I exfoliated my face last night with this Bamboo product. Check out the ingredients below! I woke up today and my face feels fresh!

(company post will appear here)

<u>Services & Others</u>

I am excited to be attending my company's convention next month. I get to meet a lot of other entrepreneurs who are helping people save money on their electricity bill. Check out the post below on the convention details!

(company post will appear here)

<u>Clothing & Accessories</u>

I love jewelry! Anyone like this new piece? See below.

(company post will appear here)

<u>Leisure & Educational</u>

Has anyone ever been to the Four Seasons? Check out the post below. A fantastic deal going on right now with them! Let me know if you have interest.

(company post will appear here)

How Often Should You Post?

Think about how often you post:

1. Post at least every other day. We recommend posting daily.

2. The best time to post is in the evenings or weekends.

3. If you post more than once a day, your posts should be more than four hours apart.

4. If you want to post three times a day, try one post in the morning, afternoon and evening.

Replying To Posts And Comments

Always reply and comment back.

When someone comments on a personal post, like or comment back. Also, send them a message. You can say, "Thanks for commenting on my post! How have you been?" The more you interact with a friend, the more they will see your posts in their Newsfeed.

When someone comments on a business post, like or comment back. Also, send them a message. You can say, "Thanks for commenting on my post! How have you been? Are you interested in trying a sample of my product?"

Responding To Your Friends' Posts

The more you interact with your friends, the more your business posts appear in their Newsfeed. Your friends will also see you as a real friend, not someone trying to sell them products each time they talk to you.

Your Facebook Newsfeed (what you see when you click on "Home") is personalized to you. It is filled with your friends' posts, pages you liked and people you are following. Only your friends appear in this Newsfeed, and they cannot see each other's post unless they are also friends with each other.

When you comment on a friend's post, write from the heart. Be yourself. Treat it the same as when you talk face to face or on the phone.

Be responsible and respectful. Many people will see your comments, so be careful of what you say.

Save Time By Using Facebook Lists

To optimize your time, sort through the Newsfeed using the lists you created on Facebook.

Prospect List: By liking and commenting on these posts, you're staying in touch with those who aren't ready to try your product. One day they may have a life experience, realize the importance of your product and ask for a sample.

Sample List: By liking and commenting on these

posts, you're staying in touch with those who are trying or have tried your product. It gives you the opportunity to build a deeper relationship, which can lead to them telling their friends about your product and become a customer.

Customer List: By liking and commenting on these posts, you're building deeper relationships with your customers. Customers who trust you are usually willing to share your product with their friends and make future purchases.

Team List: By liking and commenting on these posts, you're building deeper relationships with your distributors. Most distributors quit due to lack of support. You can now personally support your team daily as if you were working with them face to face.

If you check your lists daily, we recommend investing 10-15 minutes total.

In each list you'll see friends' posts. You have several options with each post:

Like it if you agree or think it's interesting.

Comment if you have something to say.

Share it if you think your other friends may enjoy seeing it.

Or, don't do anything. You don't have to respond to every single post.

Final Thoughts

Remember, a trusted relationship between two people is a two-way street. It's about giving and taking. Have fun chatting on Facebook. It will lead to good business.

11. Grow Your Friends To Grow Your Income

If you run out of people to talk to about your products, you run out of business. And if you aren't growing, you're dying.

New people are all around, but we struggle to start conversations with them. Believe it or not, Facebook is a solution to this.

With over a billion users, Facebook offers an unlimited amount of people to talk to if you take the time to build relationships.

With Facebook, you can connect to:

* People you may know already
* Friends of your friends
* People from your hometown
* People where you currently live
* People who went to the same high school and college
* People with similar interests
* People who use similar products

Facebook offers something called Graph Search. We call it "how to never run out of people to talk to about your product."

Graph Search is Facebook's portal to their "graph" of people and pages and interests and how they're related. With a billion members and millions of pages and affinities, there are trillions and trillions of connections in the graph. Everyone has an average of 200-300 friends, and everyone likes dozens and dozens of Facebook pages, books, movies, and so on.

To use Graph Search, type keywords into the Facebook search box.

Graph Search allows you to find people by name or phrase. Here are general examples of phrases you can enter into the search box:

* Friends of my friends
* People from my hometown
* People who currently live in (insert a town)
* People who graduated from (insert your school) high school in (insert a year)
* People who graduated from (insert your school) university in (insert a year)
* People who work at (name of your current or past employer)
* People who like (enter a hobby)
* Pages liked by people who are my age
* Pages liked by people who are over (age) years old
* Pages liked by people who majored in Accounting and live in United States

As you search for new Facebook friends, you will come across people you already know. It is best to add them as a friend and send a message. Since it has probably been a while since you've spoken to them, don't talk about your products. Reconnect only. You can share your products when they see your quality posts. The only time we recommend sharing your products is if they ask what you do for a living.

If you don't know someone and still want to be friends, try following her first. Keep in mind, not everyone has a follow button. Spend time liking and commenting on her posts. When she interacts with your comment, then send her a friend request. Once she accepts your friend request, she will see your posts.

Don't get too crazy with adding possible friends. If too many people deny them, Facebook may block you from adding new friends for a while.

People tend to accept friends based on mutual friends and common interests. That's one reason you need to fill out your profile completely and accurately.

Imagine reaching out to 10 new people a day. This should take just fifteen minutes. Every month that adds up to 300 new potential customers for your product. After a year, your Facebook prospect list has grown to 3,600.

Place those you're following into an Interest list. The Interest list works just like the Friends lists you've already created, except these people are not yet friends on Facebook. Name the lists based on the Graph Search phrases you used to find them.

Final Thoughts

The biggest reason distributors fail in direct sales is they don't have a constant stream of new people to speak with about their products. Graph Search solves this concern by opening up Facebook's entire database to you. All you need to do is take the time to reach out and build relationships.

12. How Birthday Wishes Create Business Success

How do you feel when someone wishes you a happy birthday? Better yet, how do you feel when hundreds of people wish you a happy birthday on Facebook? It makes you feel great because someone took time out of their life to recognize your existence.

Wishing someone a happy birthday on Facebook is one simple act that builds a stronger relationship. It also gives you an opportunity to start a conversation that may lead to you talking about your products or reconnecting with someone you haven't spoken to in a while.

Wish someone a happy birthday by posting on their wall or sending a private message. We love to send a private message because it creates a one-on-one conversation that might lead your friend to ask, "What have you been up to?" This question gives you the opportunity to talk about your products. By sending a private message, you are really saying, "I care about you. You are important to me. I don't want you to just be a

Facebook friend. I want us to be real friends." If you wish someone a happy birthday on their wall, you will blend in with the many others who did it as well. Separate yourself from everyone else by sending a private message.

Making it personal goes a long way.

You might say, "Happy Birthday, Dan! How does it feel to be 30?"

You may ask a question by saying, "Happy Birthday, Susan! What are you doing fun to celebrate your special day?"

You might put a personal touch to it by saying, "Happy Birthday, Charlie! I saw the picture of you and your family at the lake last week. You guys looked like you were having so much fun."

The personal touch might take an extra 20 seconds. It could make the difference in building a lifetime relationship with your friend.

Here are a handful of birthday wishes Jim has done over time. Look at these real-life responses. We added what has happened to the relationship with each of them since wishing a happy birthday.

Jim: Happy Belated Birthday!

Kate: Thanks, Jim!! I really appreciate that you thought to send me a note. Awesome!

Outcome: Jim and Kate talk more frequently on Facebook Chat compared to once every six months before the birthday wish.

Jim: Happy Birthday!

Susie: Very sweet for the personal touch! How is that gorgeous baby??

Outcome: Susie likes and comments on Jim's posts

more frequently now.

Jim: Happy Birthday!
Jennie: Ahh thanks so much!!
Outcome: Jennie writes more heartfelt comments on Jim's posts.

Jim: Happy Birthday!
Lon: Thank you! We need to connect soon!
Outcome: After two years of barely talking, Lon now wants to catch up over the phone.

Jim: Happy Birthday!
Jasmine: Thank you Jim! I have been hella busy this past month, but I logged in today and saw a ton of wonderful messages. I really appreciate it!
Outcome: Jasmine and Jim find each other commenting on each other's posts more frequently.

Jim: Happy Birthday!
Kristin: Thank you so very much!!!
Outcome: Kristin likes Jim's Facebook posts more frequently now.

Jim: Happy Birthday!
Michael: Thanks Jim. What is your business?
Outcome: One step closer to doing business with Michael.

Jim: Happy Birthday!
Sherry: Thank you. I appreciate it.
Outcome: Referred business to Jim shortly after the birthday wish.

Jim: Happy Birthday!

Greg: Thanks Jim, how are you?

Outcome: Referred business to Jim shortly after the birthday wish.

The above examples demonstrate that even a simple happy birthday will give you the opportunity to talk about your products if you've created a meaningful relationship with people by doing the right things on Facebook every day.

What Should You Do When Someone Wishes You A Happy Birthday?

It can be overwhelming receiving hundreds of birthday wishes on Facebook. Each birthday wish is an open invitation to talk about your products. We suggest sending each person a thank you message through the private message feature.

Here are examples of what we mean in the six main direct sales categories. Always rephrase these in your own words.

<u>Home/Family Care</u>

Thank you for the birthday wishes! This past year has been wonderful for my family and me. We became a customer of a 100% natural, safe home product line, ranging from cleaning products to clothing detergent. We decided to start sharing them with our friends to make some extra money. We were blessed this year!

<u>Wellness</u>

Thank you for the birthday wishes! This past year has been wonderful for my family and me. We started taking our health seriously by eating right and using different products that helped us lose a lot of weight and feel great!

We decided to start sharing some of the products with our friends to make some extra money. We were blessed this year!

Personal Care

Thank you for the birthday wishes! This past year has been wonderful for my family and me. We became a customer of a 100% natural and organic skincare line. We decided to start sharing the products with our friends to make some extra money. We were blessed this year!

Services & Others

Thank you for the birthday wishes! This past year has been wonderful for my family and me. We became a customer of a new electricity company and cut our bill by $30 a month. We decided to start sharing this savings idea with our friends to make some extra money. We were blessed this year!

Clothing & Accessories

Thank you for the birthday wishes! This past year has been wonderful for my family and me. We bought some beautiful jewelry from a direct sales company and decided to start sharing the jewelry with our friends to make some extra money. We were blessed this year!

Leisure & Educational

Thank you for the birthday wishes! This past year has been wonderful for my family and me. We went on a few vacations and saved a lot of money because of a program we signed up for a few months ago. We decided to start sharing the program with our friends to make some extra money. We were blessed this year!

You can also have a conversation with your friend first before talking about the business.

Here is one example using the personal care category above:

Samantha wishes you a Happy Birthday on your wall and you send her a private message.

You: Hey, Samantha! Thank you so much for thinking about me on my birthday. How have you been?

Samantha: No problem! I am doing well. Between work and my little one, I am keeping busy. What's new with you?

You: Busy is good, and it keeps you young. Well, I just started this organic and natural skin care business. I love how the products feel on my skin. Would you like a sample?

Samantha: Sure, I would love to try them.

We know it can take a while to reply to all of your birthday wishes, but it will pay off. No one ever said building relationships was easy. You never know what opportunities will come up when taking the time just to say, "Thank You."

Final Thoughts

It's the simple things, like wishing someone a happy birthday, that lead to more customers, distributors and referrals. Show someone you care by wishing them happy birthday, and they will return the favor by helping you build a successful business. Remember, you don't wish someone a happy birthday because you are hoping to gain a new customer. You wish someone a happy birthday because you genuinely and sincerely want to be their friend.

Remember: If you need more than the book...
Bring the book to life with diagrams and how-to videos.
Stay current with the latest changes in social media and
how it can grow your business by joining our community:
http://socialmediadirectsales.com/training

Want personal, one-on-one coaching? Go here:
http://socialmediadirectsales.com/coaching

PART II: THE INTERVIEWS

The Interviews

We are thrilled to present these new interviews from outstanding leaders in the network marketing industry! A few things about the interviews before we begin:

We love these interviews because they're filled with tips and techniques to help you succeed faster. Note that some of our interviewees have strong opinions and may even disagree with each other. We recommend you take what works for you and leave the rest.

We chose these people because they earn more than $100,000 per year in network marketing (and some of them earn more than $1 million per year). They also believe that Facebook helped them achieve this level of success.

We wanted them to be a part of our book because they understand the importance of building relationships, the silver lining of our industry and the definitive difference between an amateur and professional distributor of network marketing. They are actively involved on Facebook daily and able to connect Facebook to the overall strategy of building a successful network marketing business. Enjoy!

Karen Aycock

Karen Aycock has been a stay-at-home mom for 16 years. She started with her current network marketing company in October of 2012, and had no experience in Network Marketing. She made $7,800 in her first six weeks, sharing the product only with her close, inner circle. By her fifth month, she made a six-figure income. By her seventh month, she was an Ambassador, the company's top level. In her first year, Karen made over $140,000.

-

The Internet and Facebook
I share the company with everybody I meet, and I use Facebook to connect with people and make new contacts. At one point, I personally recruited 44 people and 26 came from Facebook connections. Most of them were high school classmates and others who were not necessarily strangers, but were people I wouldn't have connected with

otherwise—people I don't normally run into. Facebook makes growing a network marketing business very fun and profitable, and you'll find yourself connecting with lots of people!

Facebook has been a huge tool for me. It would have taken me twice as long without social media—maybe even longer. Getting distributors is my focus. I'm so passionate about the business opportunity. I believe with the company I'm in anyone can succeed. With social media, it makes working from home very exciting!

Personal relationships are the key to building a successful business. Wish them a happy birthday. Comment on their pictures. Let them know you truly care for them. Then someday it will lead to a private conversation about how my product or opportunity could help them. For instance, if they lost their job, I will share my opportunity with them. Or if they are suffering from illness, I'll let them know about my product. But the bottom line is, it's all about meeting someone else's need and helping them where they are in life. Facebook makes these relationships and opportunities priceless in network marketing.

Obstacles Overcome

My biggest obstacle was speaking in front of people and personal growth. After staying home with my kids for 16 years, meeting with new prospects and training my group was outside my comfort zone. Honestly, I had never spent much time on reading or personal growth. The first convention I attended, I was asked to share my story onstage in front 1,800 people. You can imagine my anxiety! I didn't want to go on. I cried and was nauseous, but I knew I would grow with the experience, so I got through it! I felt like I had conquered the world when I was finished! When you speak from the heart, you don't worry about being scripted. You just have to do it. Your fear will go away and you'll grow. Now, speaking and sharing my passion is just part of what I do, and I absolutely love it!

Meeting New People

I don't just go out looking for prospects. I go to create relationships.

"How long have you lived here?"

"Where are you going to school?"

"What are your goals?"

"How long have you worked here?"

"Are you interested in making part time money?"

Those are just a few examples of questions that can lead to the perfect opportunity to share what you have. You're not trying to sell something, you're trying to meet their need. Do they have a health or weight problem? Figure out what their need is. Money? Health?

I went on a company trip to Jamaica. While lying on the beach, I met a lady and her husband from New York. We started talking, and they were very interested in our opportunity. We clicked right away! They met our CEOs and several of the top leaders and immediately knew they wanted to be involved. But it all started with creating a relationship on the beach on a personal level. Now they are getting incredible results from the flagship product, and we have become great friends that I know I will have for a long time!

It's all about getting out of your comfort zone and developing relationships. The people this opportunity has brought into my life are a pure blessing!

Nurturing Relationships

To nurture relationships, always stay in close contact with new distributors and customers. Connect with customers and find out what results they are having. Let them know you appreciate them and their business. I also help a new distributor have their first party and train them on our system. I walk them through the whole process until they're comfortable leading their own group. I let them know how to launch their business on Facebook. For example, when you receive your kit, post a fun picture and let everyone know you are excited about your new business and sharing the products with everyone. It will immediately lead to your friends asking about the product and is the perfect opportunity to get everyone excited about trying your samples or coming to your first party!

What should you avoid? Just love people where they are. Some people are going hit the ground running, others just want to sign up four people to get their product for free. Just realize that not everyone has the same goals as you. Don't expect someone who only wants to give 10 percent to give 100 percent. Simply let them know they have your full support with anything they want to accomplish. And always remember to only post positive, uplifting posts on Facebook. You want to draw people to you and see you as someone they will be excited to work with!

You have to lead by example. Don't expect a new person to recruit if you aren't recruiting or expect them to host meetings if you aren't hosting meetings. Every morning, get up and ask yourself, "If everyone does exactly what I do today, will they be successful?" Lead by example. You will not only have respect as a leader, but you will create duplication that will lead you to a six-figure income!

Masa Cemazar and Miguel Montero

Masa Cemazar and Miguel Montero are seven-figure earners, have a network marketing business on five continents and have teams in over 30 countries with more than 50,000 members. Masa is from Slovenia (Europe) and has a BA and Master's degree from Oxford University and a PhD in Molecular Genetics. Miguel is from Spain and is a trained commercial pilot. He also spent more than 15 years as a semi-professional and professional soccer player. Masa and Miguel have lived in Brisbane, Australia for the past 10 years and travel frequently to support their worldwide teams.

-

The Internet and Facebook

We started in network marketing nine years ago. We were introduced by a 17-year-old girl, and at that time we did not know network marketing existed. The reason we joined was because we were looking for a different lifestyle. The Internet wasn't used as much at that time, so the good thing is that we learned basic networking skills offline. For example, we learned how to build relationships and recruit people. You need the same skills online and offline to become successful. I'm glad we "grew up" without the Internet first. When social media came into play, we could use it successfully and in an appropriate way to cast a bigger net.

Nine years ago we were not very efficient at using the Internet. We've learned to adapt and evolve with time. The industry is very much online now. We've been using Facebook to better target the audience and target what we need. You can spend hours and get nowhere, so before we go on Facebook, we get specific about our goals and plans first.

The best strategy for using Facebook appropriately for network marketing is to look for friends of friends. Through Graph Search you can choose country or market or city, look at friends of friends and start connecting with them because you have friends in common. You can look at people with experience in network marketing in a specific city or state or country and find particular people you can talk to and build a relationship with first. People often use Facebook inappropriately to hit people up with opportunities. The right approach is to build a relationship with them first and make friends before you introduce them to an opportunity. You want to find people who are looking for a better life in some way, and you can search for them via interests like personal development, investment interests and continuing education.

When we were opening the Nigerian market, we used Facebook to establish contact, warm up the market, find some leaders to rely on, and then get referrals to go deeper into the market.

We sponsored over 200 people in Nigeria before we traveled there for the first time. You fly where the volume is and develop it. You need to set targets for them. They hit them then you travel there.

We use Instagram nowadays and get lots of people looking at our website. We've started a coaching and consulting company that's for people looking to be successful in network marketing, and it's not specific to one direct sales company.

It's a total waste of time start with: "Hi, here's my company." Also, copying and pasting a paragraph from a Facebook marketing program like "I saw that we are both interested in Brian Tracy" isn't effective. If it's too generic, people know it's a formula! Remember to be yourself and be honestly interested in people. You have to create a relationship and friendship and use the same offline skills online to create success.

We use all social media as a tool to attract new people. People focus too much on generating leads. If you make a good friend you can get a team of 1000 people out of one person. Get the quality person. Make better relationships—quality over quantity. If you're thinking you need more people, maybe you need better relationships.

Obstacles Overcome

When you start in the industry, you start spending money on products, tools, travel and many other things. In the beginning, your income's not there yet—you're investing money into the business, having meetings, using your car to meet people. You have a day job paying the bills.

Our biggest learning in the nine years was how to manage our finances the correct way. We got big time into debt. We invested more than 100 percent back into the business, and we were growing the check but spending more than that. You need to be mindful that if you're growing a business in a different city or country, you will have more expenses. We learned that the hard way. We started traveling overseas and that means hotels, air tickets, food, events, and many things to spend money on, yet the income wasn't there. So we got another credit card, spent more money here and there.

Sooner than later you realize you're more in debt. The income is up, but making $10K and spending $15K on expenses is not profitable. So we had to learn to maximize our profit, investing 80 percent of the profits back into the business. Always think: where's the volume, which countries are making that volume, what kind of profit are we getting in each country, how can we reinvest into that market and travel there and make it profitable?

But you need to go through a phase in new biz. Go through a low-income phase, but invest time and money in yourself. Then as you make more money, you don't live above your means to show off. Network marketers do that a lot. When they get to $80-90K per month, people buy big cars and show through social media how much money they make, how successful they are. Yes, it's a business tool, but most people do this for financial freedom and other kinds of freedom. Financial freedom requires not enslaving yourself to debt. Don't get into debt for reasons that won't help you in the future. Invest in assets and yourself. There are wise ways to use money.

The biggest thing for a brand new person is if they can remember to save 10 percent of everything and never touch it, that's a huge plus. Don't spend more than you earn. Always save some money for yourself so this journey will get you somewhere. It's very important that network marketers don't increase expenses with increasing the income. Start thinking about assets and liabilities. Go back to Kiyosaki. Understand why you are doing this in the first place: for a residual income that will be the legacy for your family. So spend money on things that will make you money. You need a financial education and investment strategy. Even in network marketing, you have to invest money to make money. But be smart about it. Be prepared to invest 30-50 percent of commission to organize events and travel, especially at the beginning.

Meeting New People

You need to use your offline skills online. Don't take shortcuts. The danger is we want to take shortcuts and rush it. We forget to create relationships. If you take time to create a relationship with a high-quality person, you may have just created $1MM. Remember that. Slow down to speed up.

Start to be an advocate for the network marketing profession. You need to get educated on the whole profession beyond your company. Longevity with company is important. Loyalty is great. You need to get into the habit of staying in touch with other leaders. Your friend may be with one company, but they may be looking for a new opportunity in a few years' time. If you're earning $10K a month, in three years, people will be excited to see what you're doing and that you persisted on your journey.

Million dollar income takes time to develop. Be patient. Create relationships. Every company has a wonderful product. Every compensation plan is a good one. As long as you work, it works. As you grow as a leader, become an advocate for the profession and embrace other companies and differences between people.

We met a couple five years ago. They were excited but

had some family issues. They decided not to get started. They tried three other network marketing opportunities. Somehow none of them worked out. Five years later, we happened to be in their country and invited them out to coffee. We had been in touch with them for five years, we knew all about their lives and family. We just really wanted to go for coffee or lunch. Turns out <u>they</u> asked if they could work with us now.

You don't have to push people to start with you. In five years, I guarantee if you've made real relationships and positive friendship, people will come to you and sign up with you. Now, we do not sign up everyone that wants to—even our friends! We pass them to our downline. Honestly, we don't have the time to support them properly. But we do choose specific people who are willing to learn fast and work hard. So that is the difference.

Stay the course and stay focused. In five to ten years when you're successful, people will beg you to work with them. Slow down, focus on the friendships and don't be desperate. It's going to happen. Be patient and look after the people.

Nurturing Relationships

For keeping in touch, Facebook is wonderful. We check Facebook Messenger and email, relax with coffee, send ten to fifteen messages per day: how is your daughter, how was your trip, how was your birthday? Be interested, like you are with friends. Not "are you in that company still?" Just relax and be yourself!

You don't need 10,000 people to succeed. The number of people we personally sponsor that gave us 95 percent of our team, is six. We've sponsored close to 300 people, but we had to speak to thousands of people. So find a few hundred then focus on the serious ones. You don't need

50,000 people. Don't sponsor everybody. You just need the good ones. Some just rise to the top. You give everyone the same opportunity, judge people by their actions. The ones talking to people going to your events? Reward them with your time. Do presentations for them, and you'll see which ones are the top twenty.

It happens naturally. You have that gut feeling when you meet people. You have to be willing to be teachable, and then be ready to take the action. Action speaks louder than words. You don't know when you meet someone if they'll be a future leader, but you can see how teachable and humble they are, whether they have something different from the rest. It's that little edge some people have that tells you they have a bright future. When you tell them to do something, they don't ask why, they just do it. They get guidance, put it in action, and keep asking you: how can I do better?

We never questioned if network marketing success was possible. We knew it was possible because we saw people making six, seven, eight figures, and we thought to ourselves: there's something they know that I don't know that I need to learn.

If you have a personal interest that's not just business, people will stick longer with you. That will give them more opportunities to have success. You have to go through enough people to find these few. It takes time. You can't shortcut it. So relationships keep people going through difficulties.

A dangerous viewpoint is "I am unique, therefore I am better than everyone else." If you can get vaccinated from that from on day one and stay humble, you will get more chances to make it happen. Ninety-seven percent of people in this industry never make it.

Facebook is a magnifier. If you're interested in people,

it will become obvious. If you're not, that also will be obvious. Find common interests, don't hit them over the head with opportunity and be patient. If you like personal development, Tony Robbins has a huge fan page. When he posts, you see thousands of people liking his posts. All those people who liked his posts? Check them out, follow them and like their posts before even getting in touch with them. Find out what they do. Eventually send a message. They know who you are because you've been liking their stuff and they're wondering you are. Say hello and you're one step ahead of anybody else who just gets on Facebook and sends a copy-paste message about an opportunity. Those little things make a huge difference. It's what you'd like them to do if they were doing it to you.

A lot of people get into network marketing and try to find shortcuts to generate leads online. There's nothing wrong with lead gen, but go through an offline process of building relationships and recruiting. Don't waste a lot of time building a blog and learning PPC and other very complicated stuff because no matter how smart you are and how many leads you get, the real success in network marketing comes from fast duplication. Those skills are not quickly duplicable. Do things you can reproduce fast.

For example, if your company has a video presentation online, you need to get many people to watch it. That is duplicable. You can't teach them to blog and PPC in a day. Do network marketing first. Go out in your city and make new contacts. Find a lot of new people, make a lot of new friends. If you don't want to make a lot of new friends, you're in the wrong industry.

Focus on skills that make you a lot of money. PPC ads? Maybe long term, but not if you want cash flow now so you can go full time later. Don't get lost in the online world, the idea that you're going to work only online from home. Five years ago, everyone was at home online. Now it's going back to let's do a home party presentation because the results are much better. See people face to face in your house. An upline who's a good presenter could close ten people in one night.

No one country is better than another. We've been in 25+ countries, from 200 to 2000 people at events. Always, people who come for advice say, "It's so great what you're trying to teach us, but in our country and city people are negative." Where we live, we think people are negative, but it's the same in every country—Asia, Africa, Europe—we all have the same challenges. It's not just you. It's not just your country. It's a normal challenge. Build the right skills so you can go faster. All countries have amazing markets, but they can be a little different. In a developing country with slow Internet, you can't have an online presentation on a webinar every night—offline home presentations are better. In a first-world country, you're not going to just do offline home presentations—you can add in webinars.

My science background was not helpful at all. When I first came in as scientist or pilot, with a good education, a high-paying job and a certain status in society, people look up to you. People say, "It's so easy for you. The distributors in your downline can't duplicate your background or your advanced degree quickly and easily. What works for you has to work for a hundred other people. Don't become an expert. I just blogged, "Avoid Being a Know-it-all" about seven bad recruiting habits. We think we need to be experts and know everything about the company and product. It's about appearing as though you signed up today and showing others that they can do it tomorrow. If you're humble enough to understand that, you'll take off with it. It's the system, not you. You're not the message; you're just the messenger. It's not about you.

It's about the prospect knowing and feeling that they can do this.

When we go to Asia, we get treated like rock stars. You need to stay focused and humble. Your ego gets reinforced. It feels good, but say, "This is who I am, and who I'm going to stay. I'm going to stay humble." We take thirty to sixty minutes after every event just to stand up and smile so if they want to take a picture for their biz, they can. You have to stay focused on results. Make sure every message you give is duplicable, not super complicated. Attention is great, and you deserve it, same as your team does, but everyone needs to stay focused on results.

Daren Falter

For 24 years, Daren Falter has been in network marketing as a top independent distributor, consultant, speaker, trainer and vendor to the industry. He is a cofounder of a network marketing company, which launched in November 2009, and now has more than 40,000 distributors. Now in its revised sixth edition, Daren's book, <u>How to Select a Network Marketing Company</u>, has been translated into three languages and has sold over 50,000 copies.

-

At our company, we transform lives—physically, emotionally and financially.

Our company is unique in that it was founded by distributors, for distributors. Each of the five founders was successful in network marketing prior to launching our own corporation. At launch in 2009, we exploded with activity and volume, doing over one million dollars in our first month. Then for nearly two years, we experienced endless problems and setbacks. Growth was slow and insignificant. After executing a number of unsuccessful programs and strategies, we launched a collection of products. This systematized product approach pushed us into momentum growth. Shortly thereafter, we introduced our business building system, designed to promote duplication and teamwork. With these product and business systems in place, we have since experienced a doubling—even a tripling—effect year after year.

The Internet and Facebook

We love Facebook. As part of our system, we encourage distributors to use Facebook on a daily basis, not as a primary prospecting and recruiting tool, not as a primary customer acquisition tool and not to run ads for the product or business. Our distributors are encouraged to use Facebook for the following:

1. Social Proof for Products: Distributors post before and after weight loss photos and legally-compliant product testimonials.

2. BBP Invite Support: We build through parties, which are held in homes in small groups or anywhere one on one. Once an invitation is made over the phone or in person, Facebook is used to post reminders through personal message, on their wall and even through Facebook Groups.

3. Recognition: Facebook is the ultimate recognition tool. When distributors achieve a new distributor rank, receive recognition at an event, qualify for our Luxury Vacation Program, or qualify for our Luxury Car Program, pictures are plastered all over Facebook and the likes and shares go nuts.

4. Promoting Large Events: All conferences and regional events are marketed through the our Facebook page and on the walls of our distributors.

5. Social Proof for Lifestyle: Whether its distributors and customers snapping selfies at a Customer Appreciation Party or Culture Activity, someone shooting video of pool volleyball in Cabo, or a GoPro of Blue Diamonds riding Segways along the Seine near the Louvre in Paris, these pictures and videos ignite the possibilities and passions for others and drive them to pursue a career with us.

Building Relationships

There are many other ways Facebook helps us, directly and indirectly. But mostly, Facebook is a support tool for our belly-to-belly marketing. Most of our business building is through personal, face-to-face contact. This is where powerful, long-term relationships are formed.

We believe in building relationships with people. We call ourselves a family. We focus on loving one another and eliminating drama, fast. In fact, we have a mantra we use: "DKC: Drama Kills Checks," meaning if you allow drama to perpetuate in your team, you will sabotage your business. That's why our family is drama free. Well, mostly. We're only human. Some companies are so focused on recruiting and making money that when the check stalls, the people go away. I like to believe it would take more than a few hiccups in our business to weaken the bonds of our family. We just love each other. A lot.

The System

From 1995 to 2008, I did a lot of direct mail, direct media and direct Internet response advertising and marketing. I spent a lot of money, and I built some huge downlines into the tens of thousands of distributors. It all started with the AOL chat rooms in the mid-90's then moved to email list building at the turn of the century and, finally, to pay-per-click advertising on Google and other popular sites. I was huge into card pack direct-response mailings from 1996 to 2004, and then I spent several years perfecting my full-page display advertising strategy using many business opportunity industry trade publications. All of these did well, at the time. None of them work today. Besides, I got tired of killing trees. I like trees. But even in its heyday, when the cold marketing ads were pulling like crazy, the quality of those contacts was subpar. The face-to-face, warm market strategies we use today attract a much higher caliber person, and the relationships we build with those individuals are much stronger and more permanent.

We discourage our family from doing advertising, setting up a booth at a trade show, or doing any kind of Internet marketing. Not only are there issues with regulatory compliance, but building in the "cold market" with complete strangers is costly and slow. By seeing value in a remarkable product and sharing that product with your friends, family, and associates—your "warm market"—even someone new to network marketing can have positive results. We help turn ordinary people with extraordinary dreams into leaders.

Duplication

We live by another mantra: "It's not what you can do, it's what you can duplicate." Creating one of our businesses is all about replicating successful systems and strategies. It's like McDonald's. There's a reason that a restaurant chain that makes medium-quality food can have multi-billion dollar success. It's not in the burgers; it's in the system. As I've ventured into McDonald's in Japan, Singapore, Australia, Rome, Paris and even in my own backyard (strictly for business educational purposes, I assure you), I notice one thing. The system is the same. The way the kitchens are laid out, the way the drive-thru works, the way the employees take orders, the way they advertise and order their supplies—it's all the same.

We've taken these lessons from Ray Kroc home with us. Whether you come to one of our parties, trainings in my area near Seattle or go to the same event in LA, New York, or Des Moines, Iowa, it's all the same. Every event follows a certain pattern, by design. We don't want people doing their own thing. For ultimate success, simply create a system any teenager can follow and then push it many generations deep.

We have a collection of products designed to work synergistically together. They're focused on balancing the body and promoting superior health, longevity, better sleep and increased energy. But one of the most amazing side effects is that almost everyone builds lean muscle mass and loses weight. New customers join and get a kit, a 30-day product system designed to improve health fast. We don't need to focus on recruiting new distributors because we have so many satisfied customers who have visible, emotional results in their first few weeks that some of them instantly desire to share the product with others. Becoming a distributor is a natural progression, initiated by the customer.

I truly feel that in the next few years we're all going to be forced to go toward selling product first. When you have a five-to-one customer to distributer ratio, regulators realize eight percent of the volume produced by the company is done so by those who have no incentive to consume or share the product other than to promote good health.

It's A Marathon

There are two things that kill you in network marketing. One is a lack of growth—flat-lining. But more frequently, the thing that kills a company is exponential growth, or growth a company can't keep up with. It implodes infrastructure. It delays checks. It delays product. It causes doubt and hurt feelings with distributors. Fast growth kills more than slow growth. We want to maintain a steady upward momentum without experiencing a few years of explosive growth and then a plateau, or even a drop off. We've done specific things to prevent that kind of challenge.

The system we use to build must work for everyone. If a new distributor says they want to build online with replicating websites, or hand out DVDs, or set up at trade shows, or advertise, most companies bow out and allow the distributors to do whatever. After all, they're in the field. They know best, right? That's where our expertise comes in. The founders were all successful distributors in the field. We know how difficult it is to have multiple systems within the same company or even downline.

In my previous company, I was a top twenty distributor out of over one million distributors. I was happy with my success, but I saw a lot of room for improvement. So at a leadership conference in Park City, Utah, I sat down with all of the leaders who out-earned me, and I asked them how they built their businesses. Every one of them had a completely different answer. At the time I thought, isn't that interesting, there's more than one way to skin a cat. But over the next two years, I saw the negative impact this had on the company and its distributors—lots of fighting and backbiting. At the encouragement and guidance of my long-time business partner, Robby Fender (now our CEO), I sold my downline in 2008, and that's when we put together the plan to launch our network marketing company in 2009. Joined by network marketing and business legends Corey Citron, Michael Pritchard, and Bobby Jones, I took comfort in knowing we had a strong foundation of leadership.

With all five of us engaged and with the help of our top distributor leaders, we worked for several years to hone and perfect our one and only business building system. If you don't follow the system, the one system, you don't last very long. You soon find that your results will never match those of the distributors following the system. On the other hand, we still allow innovation with our top leaders. If something works well in the field, we'll research and test it then introduce it to everyone from the top down. But not until we know it is proven.

In Closing

I love Facebook. I know thousands of people on a first-name basis because of my ability to manage contacts through social media. I just wish Facebook would let me have 20,000 friends! That really is a huge issue for me. Why? Here's a great illustration. Recently I wanted to get rid of some of my 5,000 friends, since this is the cap on a Facebook account. I decided I would remove hundreds of names of people that I didn't have a relationship with so I could friend more of my distributors and contacts. I spent an hour scrolling and realized that I knew nearly everybody on the list and couldn't get rid of any of them.

Of course, we have a fan page with tens of thousands of LIKES, and I have a personal fan page (that I neglect) with thousands of likes, but there's nothing like my personal profile for connecting with people on a personal level. People don't want you droning on about business and products. They want to see how you live, what is important to you, what your WHY is all about as it is reflected in your life and lifestyle. So put your personal page out there for everyone to see. Don't post anything inappropriate for the general population and for kids. See what it can do for your business. It's amazing! Don't neglect it.

I can't give enough kudos to Facebook for what they've created—the ability to manage thousands of relationships and remember faces and names. Now, if I can prove I know them all, will you please give me 5,000 more? Pretty please?

Doug Firebaugh

Doug Firebaugh has been in network marketing for 27 years. Spanning the last 20 years, he and his team have catalyzed $1.4 billion in sales. Since 2003, his company revenues, combined with his clients' online revenues, hit over $20 million. He has what he calls an "ATM Empire," websites that continue to bring in revenue on autopilot. He has coached numerous number one earners and dozens of CEOs and company presidents. He and his partner built a team of over 100,000 distributors in eight countries during his 14 years of full-time network marketing.

-

The Internet and Facebook

We were the very first company to come out with a generic network marketing social media course back in 2006 called, "The Coming Success Storm." They were CDs about what social media was and how to use it. And in 2008, I came out with "Facebook Recruiting," which was very popular and helped a ton of people. Back then, there were very few social sites. I call social media "the accelerator" because it's accelerated everything we've done, including branding, helping clients and increasing our revenues tremendously. Whether it's search engine ads, Facebook ads, pay per view video ads, or LinkedIn ads, it's had a tremendous impact. To quantify the impact of social media would be tough because the impact has been so enormous. For a lot of our membership sites, social media has taken them well above the radar. Some things have gone viral and social media had a big effect on the sales of that.

Here are three things we recommend for Facebook recruiting:

#1 Stop pretending you're working social media if you're not. A lot of people—all they're doing is going on Pinterest or Google Plus and seeing what's happening. They're not really working their business. For a lot of my coaching students, we audited a couple days of what they were doing and the production was just not there. They're looking at new shoes or latest cool thing. Don't pretend you're working on social media when you're not.

#2 Don't have a multitude of platforms or you're rapidly dissipating your branding. Take a couple of sites. I call it your basecamp. Use one or two major social media sites that work for you. Everything else revolves around that. Maybe blast to others with Hootsuite. You have a brand where you're really unique, it feels good and you get results. I think you have to be on Facebook first then choose a secondary one. It could be niche sites that have 2-4 million people. It could be a lot of things, but I don't think you can substitute Google+ for Facebook yet. It doesn't have the apparatus to drive powerful income.

#3 It's not about you; it's all about what you can do for them. I have a saying: "You've gotta change your philosophy. Instead of I want something from you, you need to switch to I have something for you." This is not a taking thing. It's a giving thing. Everyone says you have to give your best stuff. I say go a step past that. Don't just give your best stuff. Give the best of you. Develop a relationship. People expect the best from you in your business, your content and your videos. But also how can you take a relationship in social to a new level that no one does or few do? A lot of Internet marketers have gone the extra mile. And now the big thing is talking to them on the telephone, like coaching or free consultation. Don't approach them like, "I want something from you." You see that every day. You can smell it—know what I mean? Give something away. Is it the best you got? Why aren't you giving your best? Put the best you've got into them, and later they'll see your power and credibility, as well as your content, above anybody else.

When you give away your best stuff, you're not giving it all away. You're giving away a portion of it as a seed because how many gardens are you going to have without seeds? We give them powerful information like, "Here Are The 7 Things You're Looking To Do When Recruiting Online." We'll give extreme information. We wow them. We build it out like crazy on the #1 and #2 things in that list of seven. Then we say, "If you want to take it to a new level, and you want to know about 3, 4, 5, 6, 7 plus 8, which we haven't even talked about..." I call that "Hansel and Gretel marketing." You have breadcrumbs. You give them a great breadcrumb, and they go, "Oh that's best bread I've ever had," and you give another and they say, "Wow, that's even better," and then you say, "Here's the whole loaf. It's gonna cost you, but you know the quality." It's fair. It's balanced. It deposits powerful information into a person's spirit, if you will. When you say here's the rest of it but it's going to cost you, you have integrity, it's ethical, because you've already given them info that helps them whether they buy from you or not.

If you're going to be on Facebook, you need the 3 V's: visibility, value and viability. You need to be visible every day because people won't believe in you otherwise. Visibility equals serious credibility. The more visible you are, the more valuable people will begin to see you. Valuable means you're starting a valuable relationship. Maybe even take it offline, which I recommend. Create some initial content that's valuable for their business or life or something emotional like compliments. What's valuable to them? Their family, who they are on their Facebook wall, your appreciation of their own content and ideas that will help them move their life and business forward. You have to prove yourself valuable. Then by default, you become viable as a possible coach, as someone to buy a product from, maybe even as a mentor. Many people are visible but their value hasn't been established enough to be a viable candidate for their money. If you have the three V's on Facebook, you can make a ton.

Obstacles Overcome

We teach in our class ABB (Always Be Branding). Everything you do, every word, every image is branding you, whether you want it to or not. You've got to be yourself, but you have to have a branding consciousness. Be conscious of what you're putting out there. People are looking at it. What you say is going to add or detract from your brand. Some people are just social and don't give a hoot. A lot are utilizing social media for marketing and business purposes. And they need to Always Be Branding.

You've heard you've got to be remembered, right? That's branding? We disagree. We want you to become unforgettable. Everybody needs to get to a space on

Facebook so that when they see you, they'll think of you later. It's not top of mind. It's top of heart. They're emotionally connected to you in a way they never would be with top of mind. How they perceive you. What value you can bring to them. That can happen in two to three weeks because of how social media works. Don't worry about being remembered. Your goal is to be unforgettable. Focus on the unforgettable factor and become an unforgettable you.

You need to have a social media plan, a blueprint for the week. If you spend hours on social media, make sure you're producing income or something that's going to produce revenue. We call it the 90-5-5. Ninety percent production, 5 percent social and 5 percent whatever you want to do. If you're marketing and you're in business, make sure the majority of what you do is going toward something that's going to create revenue.

Meeting New People

Building a relationship takes time, like a garden. You have products, but you've got to find out where the eyeballs are. Where on Facebook are the people who might buy it? People say Groups, but other ways are hashtags, comments, articles, videos and quotes. Finding the right people is the secret. Check out their profile and see what it tells you about them.

We have a little survey that we send. If you're a skincare client and you want to recruit people into your business, have a three to four-question survey you can send via email or Facebook Message after you've met them! You say, "Help me with this. I'd like to get your opinion." You're starting them into a funnel and they don't know it. Then you send them what you believe is a good assessment of their skincare regimen. You've already put together a series of anti-aging videos, say four 2-minute videos; now you're visible and valuable to them. You're at the beginning of being viable. The survey just takes a minute, and it moves them into a funnel. Now you can assess. You're not selling. You're sending information (videos) that contains secrets. Then you can invite them to a webinar or a Skype call. We usually use Skype because it's personal and you're talking to them, and then it's a different arena.

Then you recruit through them. You say, "We're looking for somebody in your area to help me get the message out." We've taught this to hundreds of people and it works. It attracts new distributors in a nice way, a powerful way and an ethical way. So you go to those people they referred you to and say, "So-and-so suggested we get together." I meet with them. If it's Skype, they might say, "Wow, this is really good. Yeah, I'm in."

If you get two of them in, you can email back the original person and say, "Mary and John are going to join me in this business because they see the potential for it. Thanks for the referral. Now, out of integrity I have to ask you: Do you want them or do you want me to have them?" It's called recruiting from the bottom up. We combine it with social media. It's a three-step process: get them in the funnel, go offline, and offer the upsell, "Do you want them?"

What To Avoid When Meeting New People

#1 Don't over-compliment. "I love your kids. They're beautiful! They're wonderful. They're so amazing. I mean really, really amazing." You can do two sentences of that but not 10 sentences. Don't gush or they'll think you want something.

#2 Don't give a tsunami of information right after they engage. Send information daily to someone. It's like dating, not marriage. Give them some space at the beginning. Go after many people, not just one. If you're too friendly too soon, they know you want something. If they're continuing to respond to it, great.

#3 The real power of the spotlight is who stands behind the spotlight. We call this "The Spotlight Factor." People put the spotlight on themselves. They're saying, "Don't you wish you could be like me?" Who's guiding the spotlight to people? Spotlight them. Retweet and share what you like from them. Occasionally say, "I recently met so-and-so she had an amazing video..." and tag her. That's promotion. Do it several times for someone. There are four steps: Conversation, Connect, Promote (Them), Construct (A Relationship). When you see them as valuable, they see you as valuable!

Nurturing Relationships

We have some very unique content. We want them to have access to it in a way that will be even more beneficial to them, and it may require some investment. We use auto-responders, but we also teach them to personalize videos. If I'd met you and we'd gotten to be friends, I'd send you a personal email. I call it "Facemail." I post it on your wall or send it, email or Facebook Message. It's just a one-minute thing that encourages, edifies and elevates you. "I appreciate your content and your kind words, and I wanted you to know that." Now it's a whole different level. It's a version of Skype. You're personalizing and calling them by name, you're moving into your world and moving into their home and they're moving into yours and really seeing your personality. That's a powerful way to personalize. Personalization has to happen. Auto-responders aren't enough. Set yourself apart and be unforgettable. Find out what they like and something they'll appreciate about that topic. For example, if you know they're from Nashville and something special is going on—"Hey look, I see that the Country Music Festival is going on there. Do me a favor: if you see Carrie Underwood tell her I said hello!" It's a joke but you're really connecting personally to their geography.

Carol and Garry Ford

Carol and Garry Ford have been in the network marketing industry for 37 years and have earned over $5.5 million. They've been executive managers, distributors, and owners of companies both inside and outside MLM.

Gary has been in the direct selling industry since 1977. He served on the Board of Directors of the Canadian Direct Sellers Association for 12 years and chaired the DSA Board from 2004 to 2006. In 2009, he was awarded the Ivan P. Phelan Award, which is given to one individual each year for their lifetime of service to the direct selling industry. In 2012, he received the Queen Elizabeth Diamond Jubilee Medal for his contributions to direct selling in Canada.

Carol was first introduced to direct selling in 1977. In just eight months, Carol's team exceeded 500 distributors. As the years passed, Carol climbed the corporate ladder outside of direct selling, all while remaining involved as a distributor. In 1997, Carol combined her two loves, direct selling and corporate management, when she was hired as Canadian General Manager for a US-based company. Impressed with her productivity, the company promoted Carol to International VP Sales just 18 months later, making her responsible for all North America. Carol served in three similar executive roles before retiring from corporate in 2011. Carol now offers business coaching to small business owners and enjoys speaking and training for audiences of all sizes. Over the years, Carol has coached and trained thousands of people on achieving their desired lifestyle by building a business of their own.

-

The Internet and Facebook

It's about building relationships. People are following us, and then suddenly they respond with a question or show up at an event they saw on our Facebook. It's been a bridge with people who wouldn't been there otherwise.

We do coaching and training. You need to be forever remembering what image you want to portray out there. Even if you're thinking this is for my friends and family, you put something out there that's inappropriate and their perception of you changes. Be professional at all times, but be fun too, be interesting, something you did with a child or pet. Make yourself real so people can warm up to you. Then they'll listen to the rest of what you want to share.

Obstacles Overcome

Carol: One of the biggest obstacles is learning to balance life. I used to claim I'm a recovering workaholic, but there's no recovering. It's who I am. This industry can really get a grip on you. You want to give it 24-7 because you so love what you do, and you believe in the dream. But you have to remember to keep your life in balance. Things work out a lot better that way. You get the results you want, and you don't hurt your relationships. I was the vice president of a company and responsible for all their field in Canada and the US. There were months when I was away from home more than I was home. That definitely hurt our family. I missed out on important times with our kids, who were then young adults and married or about to be. I've missed grandchildren's birthdays because of that workaholism. It hurts relationships, and you have to repair relationships. I had to give up that amazing job because my life was totally out of balance. I had to go back home. I met Jim Lupkin then. I decided to partner with somebody in a cosmetic company. Having my own company enabled me to keep better control of my schedule, and I didn't need to travel away from home as much. We did a lot of webinars and conference calls, which minimized my travel time. I got my life into balance while still enjoying this industry.

My workaholism cost me my first marriage, and I was determined that I would not allow it to do so again.

Meeting New People

Gary: We attend a lot of networking events. My main focus is on time management for network marketers. It's one of their biggest problems. They often have a job and family, and then they take on this additional business. Trying to keep all balls in the air can be quite a challenge. At networking events, I ask how well organized they are, how much more could they earn if they were better organized. We also do podcasts, blogs and webinars.

One of Carol's best friends is a gal she met at a mall event. It was a special day where small businesses had products and services on display in the mall. This gal was displaying her goods, as was Carol, promoting our business. This gal now works with me on our book distribution and with Carol on other aspects of our businesses. She has become a very dear friend of ours.

Don't push yourself on people. The best thing to do is

be interested in them. Learn who they are, what they do and what are their concerns. Then, hopefully, you can offer suggestions to help them. We did a networking event where a young guy came up after I spoke. He was quite successful in the computer industry. I spoke for ten minutes on time management stuff so he came to see me about buying my book. I asked him, "Are you in network marketing?" He said, "No, but I need to know about time management." He bought my book and asked if he could keep in touch. That's the kind of thing we do to meet new people.

Carol: Tying in with that is Zig Ziglar's quote, "You can have whatever you want if you simply help enough people get what they want." Find out what people want and help them get there.

Nurturing Relationships

Carol: Stay in contact with everyone you talk to. We put out newsletters. You have to have a follow-up system. Keep track of everyone you speak with. Many fall short by not following up properly. Who have you talked to last, when was that and when is your next time? Be systematic, but do it as a friend, not as a system where they feel like they're just another number.

Sometimes it takes months or even years before these leads come to fruition, so it's worth having a system and staying in touch regularly. For example, I met a person at a networking group, and we'd see each other on occasion at other events and just chat, but I would also email her stuff or make a call to see how she's doing. Months down the road, after staying in contact, she called me and asked, "What are you doing now? Because I'm looking for something different. Other business didn't work out, so tell me about yours." She ended up signing on, but it took months before she was even receptive. You miss out if you don't follow up. There have been numerous examples like this, some even take years to come to fruition. But I believe if you stay in touch, build a nice relationship with them and keep piquing them on occasion with something in line with their interests, eventually they come onboard, as a customer or business partner.

Gary: You have to avoid pushing harder or faster than they're prepared to accept. Find out where they are, what they need, and respond to that. Just like a coachee sets the agenda, the coach helps them reach their goals.

In network marketing, I see people mess that up all the time. They fire-hose people. In my last corporate role, I was a CEO in Canada of a nutritional supplement company. It was a good earnings opportunity for Associates, great products, and we frequently ran into people who were so eager to promote the products or the business opportunity that they just didn't listen to the prospect. They'd try to sell them products when they wanted an opportunity. They sold opportunity when they wanted products. We see it all the time. People are not listening, and they're pushing their own agenda on the prospect. Is it any wonder that some of these people start avoiding their calls?

Kathy Humpherys

Over the past 12 years, Kathy Humpherys has been trained and mentored by the industry's best. She has impacted the lives of both professionals and newcomers, financially, emotionally, and spiritually, while becoming a multi seven-figure income earner, co-creating six, multi-six and seven-figure earners in her business and throughout the industry, and building teams of over 75,000 members. A true believer in people, Kathy has been able to change the financial future of her entire family and many others who have successfully become leaders in the business world under her guidance. She puts people first and genuinely leads with passion and fire. This has led to many successes in both business and her personal life.

-

My husband signed me up in my first network marketing business. I never wanted to be a sales person. I end up being the fourth millionaire in that company. My team grew to over 75,000 people.

Everybody comes into network marketing the same

way. We were introduced to a product and the company by a good friend. We heard a lot of great stories of how the products were working for people. We got excited about the opportunity to help people change their health and give them the opportunity to create a part-time business. We then took out an envelope and made a list of people. We thought about people who could benefit from the products. We thought about the people in our lives that we would like to do business with. I realized quickly that this business was about people. If you focus more on people than you do your compensation plan or your product, you will be unusually successful in this industry.

I introduced the product to people who needed to change their health. I introduced the business to people who I thought needed to make a little extra part-time income. I wasn't overly attached to the product. I wasn't overly attached to the compensation plan. My focus was on people and moving them towards their dreams and their goals with the vehicle of network marketing. My first million was by default. The one thing I knew for sure was that this business was about people.

As I grew into a leader, building a strong, large organization, I started to receive phone calls and participate in three-way calls with leaders who asked me how I do cold markets. Where do I get my leads? How do I talk to somebody that I don't know? My first million dollars was built with my warm market, my circle of influence, people that I knew, that I trusted and that trusted me. Then I coached and mentored my people to work through their circle of influence, to work with people they trusted and the people who trusted them. Because our focus was on other people and their dreams, their desires and their goals, we were able to grow a substantial income through helping people that we knew. Therefore, I didn't have an answer to their question. That bothered me. At that moment, I realized I had a choice. I could either stay at that level and collect my check, or I could step up and make the decision to increase my skill set, be responsible and be a solid professional in this industry.

The Internet and Facebook

I've invested in myself and enrolled in some personal development skill set training seminars. Then my husband and I placed a full-page ad in a home business magazine. Todd created the ad, and the title was stay-at-home mom becomes a millionaire. I started getting calls right away! Here I am, a million-dollar earner and scared to return these phone calls, not knowing if I had the skill set to take the order. I realized that if it was scary for me after all my success, how would it be for someone who hadn't quite experienced success in this industry? It was a very valuable lesson for me. One of the most important things I learned by placing ads, reading a script and calling leads was the importance of realizing that with every lead I closed, every new person I brought into my business had a warm market and a circle of influence. So many times, I see people that start to do cold calling and generating leads, only to bring in people from those leads and expect them to get right on the phone and start cold calling and creating leads. I started to realize that for every cold lead I brought into the business, we could then tap into their warm market and circle of influence.

In 2008, we were encouraged to join Facebook. I said, "What the heck is Facebook?" There's definitely a learning curve in this industry. There's also a learning curve in social media. I used to tell people sitting in front of your computer, returning emails or spending time online was not an income-producing activity. It was a waste of time. I taught that 80 percent of the time you should be putting your presentation in front of new people. Enrolling and prospecting. This business is step-by-step diligence and persistence. There is no magical moment. There is no magical formula.

Then after joining Facebook, everything changed. We became more connected than ever with people all over the world. I think a lot of us stumbled through our first little while on Facebook. We created our account. We looked for friends. We accepted everybody's friend request. I would say to myself, "Why are we doing this? What is this for?" We stumbled through it, posting pictures, liking pages. I left that company in 2009. Then suddenly, Facebook became my connection to the industry.

I took a few years off. Then in 2011, we were introduced to Jim Lupkin and his social media platform. That's where we learned a lot about social media. Facebook can be a distraction to even the most focused, disciplined person. So many times I got on Facebook to answer messages, to send messages or to post, but I found myself getting lost, scrolling through the Newsfeed and, yes, getting distracted. I didn't build or recruit for social outbreak. I worked with Ted and Jim Moore on the back end, behind the scenes. I learned a lot from Jim and Ted.

I look at Facebook this way: your personal wall is like your living room. It's the place where you invite your friends, share fun experiences, pictures of your family and fun things that you do. I look at your fan page as your office where you do your business. I am connected with a lot of people who are in the network marketing industry—top leaders, trainers, coaches, consultants, even company owners. I am very respectful and cautious with what I post on Facebook. I know my personal wall is not the place to promote my business. Facebook is all about connecting with people, finding out about their families, what they do for a living, what they like to do for fun, and then being able to connect them or refer them to something that will benefit them. It's funny how people who never connect, never comment on a picture or like a post will send me a private message pitching me on the newest, greatest company that they've joined. I usually ignore those messages.

It's about building relationships. It's about connecting with people. I forgot that during my time I was out of the industry. As I started looking to reengage in a new business, I realized I had gotten lost in what's your product? What's your comp plan? I was just going through the motions. Our CEO and founder, Ron Williams, brought it back home to me, reminding me that the only sustainable peace in this industry is people. A lot of people forget that or never really knew it. Everything we do is about people, relationships, connection and building rapport, learning about people, who are they, what are their needs, their strengths and their goals. I see so many people on Facebook just pitching the newest, greatest shiny object, and they wonder why they don't get anywhere in their business.

One of my favorite ways to use social media is when I am going to do a three-way call with the leader. I can go to their Facebook page before the call, take a look at their personal profile, look at their pictures, see where they went to school, and see what kind of personality they have and what they like. That makes what I do so much more authentic and easier. I don't talk about me. I find out what they want so I can help them get it. Remember, find out what other people want, help them get it and you'll always be successful. What better way to find out who they are, what they like and what they're looking for than their personal Facebook profile?

My coach always said, "See what everybody else is doing and do the opposite." When people are used to being pitched and sold to, it's very refreshing and inspiring when you have somebody that focuses on you. Your family, your work, your grandmother, etc. One of the best questions to ask someone after showing them the presentation is, "What did you like about what you saw?" Then you can leave them with what they like. For example, if they say they like the product and you weren't listening and you're more excited about the compensation plan and you start talking about the compensation plan, you'll lose them. If they're excited about the opportunity of financial freedom and you start talking about the product ingredients, where it was manufactured, what it's made of, you lost them.

Meeting New People

I coach people daily on how to build rapport, build relationships and authentically connect with people every day. Here is the process: spend twenty to thirty minutes on Facebook today. Learn about people. Take the time to learn about your friends. You could have 3000 friends on Facebook. How many of your friends on Facebook do you really know? Would you even recognize their names if you saw their name somewhere? Take the time to reach out to send personal messages, to post and like on pictures and posts, be authentic, really care about getting to know your friends on Facebook. Have no expectation, have nothing in it for you. Focus totally on them and how you can serve them.

In the 12 years that we have been in this industry, we have built massive teams. We have built both of those teams from scratch, organically. When you go out to make friends or connect with an old friend, do it because you want to. When you reach out to help somebody or lift them up, do it because it's the right thing to do. We are all in networking. Maybe you need a realtor or a good appraiser. If you ask on Facebook, your friends will always suggest, share or connect you with someone that they like and that they have used in the past. We don't make money off of those referrals, we just do it because we want to help. It's a natural thing to do. I like to reach out. Maybe I like a picture of my friend's grandkids or a picture of a recent trip they've taken. I will even say, "I stalked you on Facebook. You have a beautiful family."

Using the technology available today and being connected to multiple social media tools, you have to be disciplined and aware of your environment. For example, you don't want to be on your tablet or your iPhone while you are standing in line at the grocery store or at the car wash with people. With people standing right next to you, you might miss a face-to-face connection.

This industry will always be high touch, not high-tech. Yes, technology makes it so much easier and effective to connect with more people than you've ever been able to before. Remember, it's a tool that helps you connect with more people all over the world. But face to face will always be the best way to build relationships.

Nurturing Relationships

Find mutual interests and look for special events coming up (e.g. "My daughter's getting married!"). Take notes, follow up, check back on people, and see how things are going. Are they struggling anywhere? Do you see a way to serve and to help them in times of need?

I remember when my first company announced that we

were going international. I thought, "How exciting," but at the same time, I was a little discouraged. I had just learned how to build a business outside of my own city, my own state. I didn't know anybody in other countries. So I thought, "That's great for other people but not for me." Now with social media, it's easier than ever to build a global business, connecting with people all over the world through social media platforms. Being able to connect through social media then being able to get on a video Skype call and see them live on the screen, see their personality, who they are and a little bit of their culture helps you be able to successfully partner with them in a global business. Then after building a foundation in your relationship and your business, you're more prepared to get on a plane and fly halfway across the world to meet your new business partner. It makes it so much more efficient and productive if you're able to lay the foundation through technology. After consistently connecting with people that we resonated with, people that we found a connection with building and sustaining those relationships, we are poised more now than ever to build a massive global business.

Kim Klaver

Kim Klaver holds a Master of Arts in teaching from Harvard University and attended Stanford and MIT. She has trained reps for 24 years in over 100 companies and has consistently landed in the top ten producers of every company in which she has been involved. She retailed more water filtration units than anyone in one company's history, nearly $60,000 in her first month alone. Kim and her team rose through the ranks faster than anyone else in the company's 25 year history. She founded Kim Klaver Productions in 1996. Her website now gets five million hits a month and has been featured in countless magazines, websites and newsletters.

-

The Internet and Facebook

Online leverage is great. There's a lot you can do that people don't realize. If you do a good home meeting, you can only put 10-25 people in each time. You have to clean your house, do your makeup, etc. But if you make a video of that home meeting and post it online, people can watch it 24/7 by the hundreds and thousands.

I'm more a teacher than anything else, so I have a whole bunch of audios people buy online on my site. I've learned write short stuff on Twitter and Facebook.

If you have ideas to express, like I do, a newsletter or blog or Facebook is a very good way to do it. I have a couple of Facebook pages. I'm not tech-oriented, but I write a post or two a day. Things like: "How to Find People to Talk to," or "5 Things Never to Say to a Good Prospect." I post stuff that comes from tutoring people, stuff that helps people move along further than they were before. Doing that each day has gotten people to sign up to be friends, and they listen and read and write comments. And sometimes, they buy my products or join my business team.

Three years ago, I started building a company online after 14 years of other activities. I used my Facebook page to ask people, "Would you like to find a way to never hear no?" or "Would you like to find a way to have a 100% open rate?" One way to do that is to send somebody a postcard!

You talk about opportunities, but you don't hammer on it or post links. You make an offer that's genuine but a little bit unique. People are thinking you mean email open rate, and no one gets 100 percent open rate unless your mom is your only subscriber. Many are getting only 5 percent email open rates because subscribers are getting hammered so much with offers from other businesses. You can automate postcard sending (from an online service). That approach made me the top builder in a company in just 5 weeks...out of 150,000 reps.

I like writing and expressing my take on things because I'm a teacher. If you're not a teacher, but you want to learn to educate or entertain, you can become a curator. You could decide to curate all the interesting posts about how to work from home or "What Do You Do When Somebody Says No (Or Yes)." Become a curator, find all the interesting sources, scour the Internet all day, find and post them and give the sources. Then you can learn and do and become useful. The news people are curators. They gather news and pass it on. That's what drudgereport.com and, in part, huffingtonpost.com do.

Another thing to get a following if you're new, is to show yourself in a process of learning. There's a girl who learned to dance online and got 4 million views in her first year after she did this. She wanted to learn to dance, and to make herself accountable, she made a video of herself dancing every day for 365 days. She was horrible when she started, but by day 365, she's hot, really good, and people go, "Holy moly!" What did she do? She showed her process. Now she's making money showing people how to do this. Expose your process. People love to show what they're doing, even if you don't become Madonna at the end. You could show people how to cook and how you have more time to cook now because you do direct sales.

Obstacles Overcome

People-related issues are usually draining. People who quit, people who become negative, etc. Today, I've become pretty oblivious of my upline. I just go for it when I decide to do something. I've had uplines quit. I've had uplines who were influential and went to other companies and cross-recruited. That's not fun. I tend to be very self-reliant. I believe I have to be my own pillar of strength, so mistakes or catastrophes don't last for me. I just try figure out what I can do.

Loyal uplines and downlines are great, but you have to make it work whether you have them or not. You have to take responsibility for being a top producer. Market the product, make sales on the product and sponsor people. And learn constantly what anyone is doing that's working. You are responsible for your success, no one else, and no matter who they say is running it—even if that person is a celebrity.

There was a network marketing company Donald Trump was part of and everybody said, "Let's go in because it's Trump!" A year later it was gone. One reason is that Donald Trump isn't going to come home with you to do the presentation. You have to do it. So it doesn't matter who your upline is. Keep asking and asking those who are getting the results you want. It's a numbers game until you find the leaders and then you tell the leaders, "It's a numbers game until you find the leaders." Leaders are made in the process.

I became a leader because I took responsibility. I had a Christmas card route at age eight, a paper route at age ten, and I organized all the paperboys. I like to run 20 lemonade stands, not one. It begins and ends with you. Don't expect anything. Be able count on yourself, first and foremost. I've trained thousands who cried their eyes out because their upline or downline left. The only answer is: start over. Everyone who's ever made it has been there. Fast success stories always have a story behind the story. This is a promotion business. The Internet is special because you can promote a webinar and give useful information. Here's what I learned on my way to becoming a top producer in our network marketing business: people will tune in because they like to see people trying.

Nothing has wiped me out (yet) because I know that "If it is to be, it's up to me." The only thing you can count on is your energy, your vision, your determination and who you decide you want to turn into.

Tip: Always read books online and off from those who inspire you. Take an author as a mentor or watch their videos or listen to their audios. Fill your mind with thoughts that make you bigger, better and more generous and forgiving. That will attract others to you.

Nurturing Relationships

Nurturing can be counterproductive. Sometimes being a teacher works to my detriment. About 80 percent of the industry are women. Women tend to be (often) like Mother Theresa. You have three people and you want to do calls with each, to motivate each one. It feels good, but it's bad for the bottom line. People who want the most handholding historically do the least and are the biggest pain in the butt. I don't mean the people who call you for, "How do I do x, y, or z?" or "Where do I fill in the form?" Those are fine. But the ones who say, "My sister said no. What do I do now? I don't think this is for me…" and want to have a cry session. Those people aren't going to do anything.

If you want it more for them than they want it for themselves, it won't work. Parents wants their kids to have a better life and more opportunity than they had. But sometimes, in our businesses, we women tend to handhold too much. Nurturing can go too far. I've fallen into that trap a lot because I like to teach. I couldn't tell the difference between people who wanted to be entertained (which is why I started selling my training) and the people who performed and brought in new customers or reps. Are you getting people on calls and you're teaching, but nobody is doing anything? Then put a price tag on the audios. Tell them they can get them for $9 to $19. But for your downline, I just give it to them. I record all my calls

132

with downlines and give it to them free. But charge if you go into teaching outsiders.

Don't nurture too much. Help them build. People quit because there's no money in nurturing alone. If you're doing therapy, you won't make money. People for whom you do therapy don't usually bring in customers and sponsor people.

Most of my teaching is motivational. My book in 1996 was totally motivational and funny. It got into <u>Success Magazine</u>. I use inspirational stuff. There comes a point where coddling people doesn't help them perform. We all need inspiration and motivation. The more you coddle people, the less they produce. You need to have or get your own internal motivation. If you take someone on steps they didn't expect to take and you're right there with them, they'll say, "Oh my gosh, I just did that!" That's the reason for going "two by two," the saying from Jesus's time. Don't forget to shake off your dust on the way out the door. People forget to shake the dust off after the prospects that aren't right. They teach elephants by yoking one to another. The new elephant thinks, "This doesn't seem weird because he's doing it, so maybe I can do it, too." That's how the sales process has been done: two by two, especially in the belly-to-belly area.

Meeting New People

I'm using Facebook ads now. In the Power Editor, you can create very specific ads to specific audiences. You can get very, very, very, very specific, and it's relatively inexpensive. If you aren't willing to or can't spend money, you can do stuff free, but it takes a lot more time. You always pay with either money or time.

Learning Facebook ads is quite a trip. You can choose an audience that's already in sales, making more than

$50,000 a year, then offer them something like, "If you could double your income with something on the side…" Then you get people, none of whom say, "It's too expensive," or "I can't sell," because they have an income, and they are already in sales. :)

It's beyond stupid to tell people network marketing is easy. I don't know a single profession that says, "It's easy!" If that's true, then why do 95 percent of people drop out? It's a giant fallacy. Most people in network marketing aren't making money. My first year in my current company, I earned $250K net, just working it online. Most don't know what to do. They were told it's going to be easy, but nobody who achieves anything thinks it's easy. Steve Jobs didn't think like that. Bill Gates didn't think like that. Peter Thiel (cofounder of PayPal) didn't think that way. Nobody who wants to accomplish anything goes into a new area thinking it will be easy. We've shot ourselves in the foot with this for the last 30 years. Masses who drop out end up blaming themselves for not being able to do it. Relating to people and making sales is not easy. Without sales you make no money. Many in network marketing deny we're even in sales. "We're sharing!" People who've never been in business get this idiotic idea that it's like recommending a restaurant. You get a potential buyer excited and they say, "I'd like try this. Where'd you get it?" And you have to reply, "Well, um, I sell it." That's a big trust-buster.

Sales is not easy. That's why few people are entrepreneurs. You can accomplish such marvelous things. You can transform yourself into a completely new person, like a caterpillar to a butterfly. Once you break free, there's no going back. But telling people it's easy? You set up the wrong expectations.

I don't recruit like that. I have 10 people I talk to online. Nine out of ten of those sign up, and they sign up for the biggest package I tell them they should get. I don't look for massive numbers to wait for leaders to come, because I've performed them properly and am always ready to say "no" first. The people who are ready for a challenge and a change sign up. And some of them do great things. Others (most) do little but enjoy being part of the group.

I'm now doing Facebook ads, and it's a targeted numbers game. Even there I'm going to qualify them with income and background. The industry is already too full of people with no money who can't sell.

Don't you want people who LOVE sales and marketing? And who love to add value to the lives of others with what they have to offer? That's you, right?

Dorina Lanza

Dorina Lanza was a Blue Diamond Executive, which is her company's top pay rank. The average income for Blue Diamonds then was $75,000 per month. She climbed to the top of four network marketing companies and grew downlines of 50,000 people. She was on the distributor advisory board, has been a keynote speaker and was named one of the top generic trainers in MLM by <u>MLM Insider</u>.

-

I started doing direct sales in 1992. In 1996, I had 1,000 people in my organization. Korea opened for business, and we went from 1,000 people to 10,000 people in nine months. You generally don't get that kind of growth unless it's a new market or new company. At my network marketing company, I had 12 strong downlines, each with their own strong businesses. It's about the people I brought in and what they did and the people I coached and worked with. Many were making six figures a year. I'm now retired, and I do private equity, coaching, and training.

The Internet and Facebook

The bulk of my downlines were built before the Internet. However, I built a series of training systems to take advantage of the new Internet paradigm, leveraging its ability to connect people and the ability to attract people online. I transferred what I'd been doing in person onto the Internet, and it worked for myself and people I coached. You have to build your brand identity, be consistent and become an attractor of people. Social media lets you do what you need to do in person but with a much broader reach.

To do this, distributors need to figure out what's important to them and who they are at the core level. I have a number of assessments I've created to help them figure out who they are and what they really want. Who you are tells you your ideal person to attract. One of the biggest mistakes people make is "throwing up all over people." You can't solicit them prematurely—it just repels people. You must build the relationship with the right people.

A network marketing business can be built with just a small category of people. If I figure out that my ideal people are 60-year-old former ski instructors who are former rocket scientists (people like me), I can easily find 12 of them and help them build. But each person you bring attracts a different type of ideal person, so you end up with a diverse and robust organization, which is good. Focus on the getting right people for you, not just anybody who can fog a mirror or anybody with a Facebook account. For example, for me, I can't attract housewives. I come down like a ton of bricks, and we just don't jive. But for others, the housewife is the ideal person.

You have to put yourself out there properly. After I did

that, they found me. My ideal people want to work with me. Sometimes they find me through wine tastings or through Beta Gamma Sigma, which is the biggest business honors society in the world. One of my key people found me on LinkedIn because I'm the founding president of Beta Gamma Sigma in Boston. He became a great client as a result.

To do this well, you want to project a consistent image in your look, how you sound, how you dress, what your website looks like and how you post on the Internet. Learn who your people are. Then use your personal and social media presence to build.

Don't just throw spaghetti against wall and see what sticks. There's a lot of bogus training that tells you to beat up your relatives and "throw up on people" online. The shiny object syndrome is also something to totally avoid— things like the latest hyped-up MLM course. Define your ideal person then present yourself in a way that will attract them. Forget about the "conventional wisdom" of this being a numbers game. It is not.

Obstacles Overcome

The biggest obstacles are self-imposed but many do not recognize them. To find them and eliminate them, personal development work must be done.

Other obstacles come in the form of doing what your upline tells you to do. They tell you to make a list of everybody you know, invite them to look at a video (and all of these videos are the same), follow up with a three-way call and other stupid stuff.

Most of the successes in this industry aren't teachers. They don't know what they did to succeed. I'm a ski instructor because I not only ski very well, but I can teach people, too. Many ski well but can't teach it. Top network marketers get to the top of their company, and they don't know why they made it. They'll say, "I talked to a bunch of people, so you should, too." But that wasn't the key success factor. This is not about throwing spaghetti against the wall and seeing what sticks.

The worst network marketers get on Facebook or LinkedIn and connect with you and the first thing they do is spam your wall or inbox with their opportunity. They haven't even said hello. That's a huge mistake. That just repels people like there's no tomorrow.

Luckily, I didn't make any big mistakes, but I wish I'd understood what I now understand more quickly. For too long, I did not understand the value of personal development. To make this business grow, you need to have certain characteristics and one of them is leadership. No one is going to follow if you're not leading. You're not going to lead from behind. You have to do that personal development work to lead. My personality has changed completely over the last 20 years as a result of this endeavor in network marketing. I had to go through that personal development process. As a result, I've become more empathetic to people. I've really chilled out a lot, too. I don't get upset. I now let people come to me.

When somebody says no, I don't freak and say, "Oh my gosh, they're so stupid! How can they not see this opportunity?" I spent a lot of time being pissed off instead of looking at myself and understanding what to do to bring in the right people. I learned that this business is appropriate for some people and not for others. In the past, I was trying to bring in the wrong people. And I was trying to bring in people inappropriate to me. I couldn't relate to them, and they couldn't relate to me. I could have been selling gold at a dollar per bar but they wouldn't have bought it because of our incompatibility.

Meeting New People

One of biggest mistakes people make in meeting new people that they could turn into buyers or distributors is that they look at them like they have dollar signs stamped on their foreheads. You've got to get to know them first. If you happen to find a problem you can solve via your product or business then solve it, or if they ask what you do, then tell them. But let them ask. Let them make the first move. If you're giving free stuff, it's not valued. They value stuff that's harder to get, that they understand they want—"Oh my gosh, I've got to have this!"

Also, recognize that people don't join network marketing companies just to make money. Some join for a circle of people to be friends with. So there are a big variety of problems you can solve. It's not all about the money. Some hang around without making money. They come to every convention just to see everybody. Some people I meet in passing come back because they felt a good vibe from me. They want to work with me. I'm attracting without asking. One said, "Oh, I've been waiting to work with you for so long," and I'd never mentioned it to her.

Nurturing Relationships

First of all, there has to be a bond, and you've got to make sure they're the right people. Some people you'll never become friends with. You can't do this in a blanket way. You've got to develop leadership in yourself so that people have something to follow. And to do that, you need to know where you're going, what the end results look like, and what style of business you want to have. You need to know what types of people you want in your business because you'll be working with them very closely, day in and day out. If you're just looking at people as entities that you'll make money on, you'll never get anywhere.

Everybody I'm in business with has become a friend. You can't tell where the business ends and the friendship begins. I think that's very important because you want strong bonds. You want people to join you. When I was building, I wasn't selling, "Oh, you gotta join my network arketing company." You want them to say, "I want to work with you." They're joining me, not the company. That's the case with every top earner I know.

You have to know what you want to create and what it's going to look like. That way you'll know who to bond with and nurture and spend time with.

Back in the Korea days, when my group went from 1,000 to 10,000, I also shot up to Blue Diamond in nine months. People would come up to me and ask, "How did you do it?" A lot of top network marketers answer that question, "Well, I worked really hard and talked to a lot of people, and I took a lot of notes." That might be true, but that's not the real root. The only thing I could tell them was, "You need to become an attractor of people." But I needed to be able to explain that better. Thanks to the Internet, I found all kinds of pieces from different fields like psychology, marketing—even investment banking, believe it or not—and I was able to put together and articulate what you need to do to become an attractor of people.

For example, I met this gentleman on Facebook, and we talked about this and that. We were doing some peripheral marketing work together. He asked, "What are you working on?" and I mentioned some international work I was doing. He said, "Okay, fine. Talk to you later."

A few months later he calls and says, "Hey, remember that international stuff? Well, I got a whole bunch of people who want to get involved in that along with me," and BANG this new business relationship came out. Why? Because we had a decent relationship and we kept in touch. And then, all of a sudden, something happened, and he said, "Aha, I need Dorina!" We talk every day now, and the business is exploding.

Another gentleman found me on LinkedIn. He calls me up. He's an accountant at a major firm. Initially, I did not think he was my style, but he was a wonderful guy. He was in an MLM and thought he wanted to build that. I would say, "Are you sure you want to do that?" We were cordial and friendly. He'd call occasionally and we'd chit chat. I didn't push him. I did more attraction-type stuff, and suddenly BANG, he becomes client. In addition to being a CPA in a major firm, he's now in a more appropriate network marketing company.

Another woman I met many years ago thought it would be nice to do something together, but she couldn't figure it out. When one of our new product systems came out, she said, "Oh my gosh, I want to come in and work with you!" But it took years. You just never know.

So my advice would be to relax and stop being in such a hurry. Do the work you need to do to let people come to you. Attract them. Hire a coach to help you get the clarity that you must have to be successful. Learn how to attract the right people. If you do this properly, you will find yourself attracting people, not only offline but online, and your reach will spread around the world.

Jill McCarthy

When Jill started her most recent direct sales business, she brought on over 270 front-line team members in six months. In one year, she had over 800 team members with over 3500 unique visitors to her website/blog. By 2013, they were quickly a million dollar (and more) team. Jill was her company's top recruiter in 2014 from January to April. Although doing more than one direct sales business is sometimes frowned upon, Jill has used online marketing to become successful with two companies, paving the way to show people it can be done—especially using social media. She has stayed firm in following the listed ethics from the Direct Sales Association, keeping the business from each company separate, and become a social media strategist in the direct sales industry, speaking at dozens of trainings for other consultants.

The Internet and Facebook

I decided to use the traditional party plan platform with a huge part of the Internet and social media as my main focus to reach more people across the US. My blog has allowed me to create a place for people to go to get questions answered, and social media has really helped me build relationships. Because of those relationships, both my team and my prospects trust me. I have allowed them into my life, to see my family, to watch my puppies grow up, and they feel that they know me. I stopped using social media for selling and started using it to build friendships, share my passion for my business with people and focus on what the business could provide for people's lives.

Now I have created a brand and name for myself in the direct sales industry. I have opportunity nights using Facebook and chats using Twitter. I motivate people to have confidence using Instagram and help with tons of business ideas using Pinterest. Being consistent across all platforms has shown people that Internet and social media can be very beneficial in being successful in direct sales and network marketing. The key has always been spending time getting to know people and letting them know how important they are to your business instead of constantly pushing a product down their throat.

I would avoid trying to be in all places online if you can't be consistent. It is better to be in one place and excel than to be on five platforms and never have any conversations. I would also completely learn the party plan platform and the company before relying solely on Internet marketing. Not everyone will do online marketing well, so we need to know all aspects of the industry to teach other team members. Many do not do that and their team is missing a big piece of the puzzle.

Decide where you are online, get really good at that platform first then move on to another. Also, really switch gears and use their online presence to spend time getting to know people and what they do instead of constantly pushing ideas, thoughts, services or products in their face.

Obstacles Overcome

The biggest obstacle has been going against the grain and using social media to build my business when others have constantly told me that I could not build a solid business using it. People have blown me off and even insulted me and how I have done things. When I ignored most of what "the big guys" told me, I was also in the middle of an abusive relationship and trying to find ways to get the courage to get out. It isn't easy to try new things, going against the grain, and to have everyone telling me that it can't be done.

I felt like everyone was against me. People have the impression that online marketing for any business is easy. I felt like I was on the outside, like I wasn't a part of the crowd.

I truly believed my way would work, and I kept plugging away. I found mentors I trust who believed in me and kept pushing me in the right direction.

I tried to fit in and wasted energy convincing people of "my way." Eventually, I just decided to prove it.

Meeting New People

Listen rather than talk. I find out their whys, what pushes them to do better or be better. I don't just sign people up. I get to know them first, and I let them talk.

Quantity over quality is the wrong way to go. When people just go after numbers instead of relationship building, trust becomes an issue and retention is simply horrible.

My career when I first started was negative. I was so consumed with just signing people up. I spent no time with anyone and the "active" numbers showed that.

145

Nurturing Relationships

I follow up and do one-on-one coaching calls. I make people feel important. I talk to them, and I listen to what they need. My entire why has now become helping women and business owners believe they can do anything.

Because of how I nurture my team, they actually created a Facebook page. They do nothing but post things daily of how much they love me. It's the smallest things like that that are worth more than ANY amount of money, ever.

Reach out. Become part of their lives and, most importantly, pay attention. Remember milestones, send hand-written cards and let them know that you are a better person because of them.

I saw how my friendships, relationships and business changed when I changed my mind-set from selling online to changing people's lives online. :) Watching those smiles, making those dreams come true, helping people believe they can do it is more than I ever thought I would be able to do for people.

Jason L. Scott, 1st

Born and raised in the projects of the Bronx, Jason Scott grew up with single mom on welfare. At 14, he brought in additional income to support his Mom by buying items at wholesale and selling them at retail on the streets. Jason is a former paratrooper for the US Army, a blue collar factory worker and machine operator. He's been self-employed for the past 20 years. Since that time, he has built teams of more than 20,000 people and personally influenced and coached another 40,000. Jason developed a 4-Step Success System to help his organization build a team of over 10,000 people in just two years. He was put on the personnel payroll by the CEO of a two-year upstart network marketing company to personally coach and mentor their entire field.

-

In December 2013, I launched a major category creator in MLM and chocolate. The first year, I came by myself and built a completely organic, international team in over 25 countries and an enroller tree (from me down) volume of a million dollars every 90 days in a year and a half.

The Internet and Facebook

The Internet played a major role in the growth of my organization. This entire company launched into Europe into the tens of thousands of distributors because of Facebook and Skype. Social media allowed me to be high tech in finding new international partners, but also high touch through free, international web conferencing through Skype. My results have been incredible. I took a quick 20 minute Facebook training Jim Lupkin gave me after I met him at a conference. I then hired his company for a month to help me manage my account and find and connect with new friends. I'm now in over 25 countries and growing because of social media.

I believe people should avoid spending all of their marketing capitol on lead generators. I'm not saying you can't use additional ways to find people occasionally, but social media provides an influx of new people to add and talk to every day. As long as you build relationships then take the conversation offline, your well should never run dry.

Obstacles Overcome

The mind! As with the majority of people, the inability to stay focused long term until success, staying focused past your have-to's until they become your want-to's, has always been a challenge.

When we "have to," we are easily distracted with life and other non-essential elements. Any excuse is a good excuse, or as they say, any excuse will do when you have to do something you don't want to.

When we "want to," daily activity becomes a MUST, and we don't allow simple distractions to take us off course. Want-to is everything. It drives us. What you are seeking is seeking you, and when you're seeking and focused, success finds you. I call it learning to go through the motions with the proper emotions!

In December 2007, I watched my mother, Thelma Veney, as she passed away from cancer, and it rocked and devastated my world. Like Lincoln said, "All that I am and all that I ever hope to be, I owe it all to my mother." Her passing sent me into a state of deep depression. For two years, I found myself unable to self-motivate. My mind and heart felt connected, and I was mind and heart broken.

After two years of basically drifting and going from building that huge team, from high success, I found myself going to the bread lines for food to feed my family. One day, two years to the date of my mom's passing, I just yelled out, "Mom, I'm sorry!"

I had promised her I would take care of everyone when she passed, and I couldn't even take care of myself. I made a commitment out loud to her that I was going to get off the couch and lying in bed all day and get my life back in order.

I started to get my life back, but it was slow and steady for several months. Once things picked up, I got a call saying that my younger brother had drowned at the beach in South Carolina. I was devastated. I promised my mother I would help everyone after she passed, and I had not even carried on the proper relationships with my siblings to ensure their well-being. I realized that was life, but my feelings of regret came from not holding true to my promise to my mother in a swift and timely fashion.

I tried to get myself engaged after my mother's passing but after my brother's death, I haven't stopped. I realize to my core that we don't know the time, day or hour we may leave this plane of existence and legacy isn't just a word for me. Legacy is my passion, my purpose.

My purpose is to strengthen the will of others. Benjamin Disraeli said that nothing can resist the human will when we risk even our very life to achieve our purpose. I teach others not to focus on the outcome but to focus on their purpose.

Meeting New People

Believe! When turning people into customers or distributors, it's your <u>belief</u> that influences people. People buy you and your leadership, not always the company. When they don't believe you, they won't buy or join you.

Tip: Faith and Action beat Tentative and Excuses.

Example: When I launched this newest project, I started financially broke, and with no team, I earned $3000 my first 15 days. I had $500 left after I paid a few bills. I withdrew the $500 (just in case another bill collector took it!) and I hit the road, traveling cross-country to Texas from North Carolina to launch the businesses of the 12 I sponsored through social media. I turned that leap of faith into well over $100,000 in earned income in the first year, but I also personally coached four others to a six-figure income, as well as thousands, to earn some incredible part-time and full-time incomes working for themselves, working from home. Don't try— <u>Do!</u> Being tentative has no power. When we are tentative, we are vibrating in this universe. It's weakness, and this is a universe that does not favor the timid!

Avoid second-guessing your abilities and potential. All that we need is within. Stop worrying. Worry causes fear and fear becomes crippling.

Example: I've sponsored, on several occasions, two or more reps at the same time, and I always see one do worse because of self-imposed limitations. I'll give the same instructions, but the ones who start off with, "Yeah, I understand what you're saying, but the people I know are different…" or "I'm just the type of person who has to learn all there is to know first because the type of people I know will want to know if I know it all before they will follow me…" are limiting themselves. There is no end to knowing it all because experts still have been learning after 20 years in the industry. The newbies who are still studying after 20 days never get off the ground.

Don't think, just trust your mentor and DO! Mentorship is wisdom without waiting.

Nurturing Relationships

The secret to mobilizing people is engaging them in the process. Getting people involved evolves the relationship. The key is to involve them by directing them and not dictating. Directing is a function of the heart. It's trust that will yield long-term results. Trust comes from the actions you take with them, not the actions you tell them to take. People will do more for you when they are getting feelings from you and feeling for you and know you have their best interest at heart.

I always ask to give me 1 percent of your trust, and I'll gain the other 99 percent.

Avoid making your relationships with your customers or reps too personal. I'll let your conscience guide you on that, but you want your people to maintain a high level of respect and trust in you, your integrity and your abilities to lead them.

We have a saying in MLM. All negative goes up and nothing but positive goes down. When negative starts to go down or cross line it pulls others down.

We all have influences in our lives. Kids, spouse, friends and others can take you for granted when they get too comfortable and can sometimes be disrespectful.

The same way you would have a problem with them being disrespectful towards you, always check yourself. A huge mistake many make is getting too comfortable with their sponsor, mentor or leader and no longer valuing their worth. Always commit to your personal growth, and you will learn to be more aware. Self-awareness and personal growth maximize your human potential and are critical in long-term MLM success.

Always remember: given the sum total of all your decisions, you can't change who you are, but given New Life, New Vision and New Unity, you can change who you become. So today, just… BECOME!

Michael Stotts

Michael Stotts has a BS in Computer Engineering from Jackson State University and a MS in Computer Engineering from Howard University. Michael received a baseball scholarship to play Division I baseball at Jackson State (JSU). He went on to work with other Fortune 500 companies such as AT&T, Siemens and Cisco Systems. After 17 years in the telecommunication industry, he retired and began his career as a Realtor professional. In April 2011, Michael started with a network marketing company. Within three years, he reached the top— Diamond. He is in the top three percent of network marketers in the world.

-

The Internet and Facebook

The Internet has played a major role for us. We can impact people at a drop of the hat once they hit social media. Whether I post or someone else does, it shows our success and impact. Testimonials attract people. We do Instagram and Facebook. On Instagram, we find a younger generation: teens between 16 and 20. They spend a lot of

153

energy on Instagram. We post on Instagram first and segue it to Facebook. I get immediate responses from Instagram. I see traction in that age bracket.

The sales that are Internet-only are small, probably about five percent. We have it as an outlet for people to go to ecommerce sites to shop, but more and more people are making belly-to-belly contact through coffee tasting parties, sporting events and church activities. There, people can touch the product, taste it and sample it. That does better than just the Internet alone.

In between the parties, people use the Internet. When we post on social media about the coffee parties, people come to the event. Whether it's a networking event or coffee party, business partners market on social media to get people there.

They don't have to come to the event because we can use the Internet to show them information about the company. People reach out to me via Messenger after they see our posts for events. They want to hear more about the opportunity. Now I can send them a link to the information or to YouTube. Then they come back to messenger and ask questions.

I use Facebook, personally, to spotlight activities going on where I'm traveling. I post about those activities with new team members and existing business partners to show successes outside the local market. It triggers people and piques their interest. They get excited and want to be a part of that success. They're just seeing stuff happen, and people naturally want to be a part of great things happening.

Internationally, we can showcase activities taking place in their local market. I'll do webinars with them or send them to training videos in our back office. I do coaching via webinars and Skype.

My advice is that network marketers in social media should avoid being non-professional. Social media is so powerful that, unless you're in front of that person and they can see your eyes and body posture, they'll make a judgment about who you are. You really have one time to project the right message. So I tell people, at all times on Facebook, maintain professionalism and avoid politics.

Obstacles Overcome

The biggest obstacle I've overcome is increasing the size of my dreams. We know desires are the root of achievement. When I came into the industry, I already had corporate success. I had already achieved a lot of my original dreams. I had the house, the cars and the clothes, so I had to learn to dream bigger. I had to create a new desire to create more activity. I wasn't getting results in network marketing because I wasn't doing the activities with momentum and a sense urgency.

The biggest thing was really believing that network marketing could be a profession for me. It was just a side thing I did as a computer engineer. It wasn't until the past three years that I began to understand this is a true profession, and it's a real business.

When I wasn't getting anywhere, my emotions were never negative, but I needed to get better and develop the skills because I already had a nice lifestyle. I needed to find the right leadership to develop my skills in this industry.

What got me over that obstacle was the caliber of leadership I've encountered in my company. I stepped my game up so I could get into that circle. In this industry, advancing higher avails you to different information. At higher levels of leadership, there are things you learn that can benefit you outside of the company from a business perspective. I aspired to be in that circle. My inspiration was to grow in the business and grow personally to get into that circle. People of pinnacle leadership have a different mind-set. The bar was so high, I had to increase my desire and skill set to get into that environment.

Meeting New People

In meeting new people, my number one tip is: be a friend. People do business with people they like.

My thing is to always build a relationship first. Then they're more open to trying your product or hearing more about your opportunity because you built that relationship.

I have a neighbor in our community, just seven houses down from me. We've seen each other for three years. I have sign on my car that shares what I'm doing, but I've never talked to him about it. I just focused on developing a friendship. More recently, we got to talk. I was able to find out more about what he does. He's very well off, a successful business man. We started to build a relationship, and he wanted to know more about what I do. My business partner and I had an opportunity to sit down with him and discuss what we do and how we impact individuals in this industry. I wasn't trying to get him to join, I was trying to develop a friendship.

When you meet new people, avoid "throwing up" on them with your opportunity. Business people can smell blood when someone is hurting. They can smell when you're a rookie in network marketing. Avoid trying to get your opportunity out there. Build relationships first and once you have a level of trust, they'll want to find out more about what you do.

Early on in my career, I was so excited. I thought everyone needed to be a part of it. But not everybody wants financial freedom. Some people, if there's not a guaranteed income, they're not interested in it. I sat down recently with a sharp young man. He said, "I've been listening to everybody else's story of what they achieved, and no one's listening to my story." As I shared my mentor's story and photo in a magazine with him, it turned him off. He thought they were flaunting their success, but really it was showing people, here's where I was, here's where I am today, and you could have it, too. So instead of taking time to interview him and ask where he wants to go, I did it the wrong way. Now I'm taking the time to build a relationship with him outside of network marketing. He didn't join, but he likes the product, so now I'm building a customer. Maybe two to three years from now, he'll be a part of what we're doing.

Nurturing Relationships

To nurture relationships, stay in touch with them and learn more about their families. What do they like doing? Know their children and spouse's names—any nuggets you can hang on to so they feel they're more than just a number to you. They're a person you care about. People don't want to know how much you know until they know how much you care. I'm always looking to build those relationships. When people aren't having success in the opportunity, the relationship is the glue that will keep them around, until they have that breakthrough, financially. I've reached out to people outside of Fort Lauderdale if their birthday pops up. You can track their birthday, new additions to family, anniversaries. Facebook has given me great opportunities to rekindle relationships.

In existing relationships, a mistake is not reaching out. You can get too busy to reach out to people. Some people drop through the cracks. A person that seems insignificant when you're growing new legs of business, you forget to reach out to them. We're in the business of people. People are the most important because they're the ones who move the product. I do self-correction. If I don't reach out or haven't given them attention, that hurts the relationships and some people will let you know. You have to give them face time. Some people you can just get on the phone with. Everybody's different. Some people are just Facebook people and love Messenger. Some people want just two minutes on phone to hear your voice and know that you care and not feel like a number.

We have 6,000+ people in the organization around the world. We have only personally referred 84 people, ten of whom I touch base with personally. Through them, I'm able to touch the others. We utilize conference calls to communicate with our plugged-in leaders. Whatsapp has been a huge tool for communication. Whatsapp is the easiest thing to get people to stay consistent with. A lot of people are still not on Facebook or don't use it enough to communicate. It's easier for me to Whatsapp people, and they respond right away. Plus, when I'm traveling internationally, I can get information out ASAP via Whatsapp.

My mind-set is that despite the product and commodity, it's all about the people. It's about developing those relationships and really finding out what people want in their business. I tell people to sit down with the newest team members and do a game-plan interview to understand what they want. People want something different than what you want. If you push them the direction you want them to go, it could hurt their career in network marketing. It could be painful for them. If they just want $500, not $5000, then you don't push them toward $5,000. It saves them, and you, time and heartache.

Kirby And Cindy Wright

Kirby is the former VP of Marketing for a network marketing company and has recently transitioned to the field, building as an independent consultant with his wife, Cindy. They are the fifth top money earners in their company and are currently earning over $500,000 per year. Before Kirby got involved in marketing, he was an electrical engineer and Cindy has enjoyed the privilege of working the business and staying home to raise their two daughters. They've been married for 31 years.

The Internet and Facebook

Kirby: Facebook has played a big part in the growth of our business. Most of the leaders that came into our business came from Facebook. Most of them watched posts for a long time then asked Cindy about the flagship product. Cindy private messaged them through Facebook and gave them a little information to see if they were interested. If they were, she sent samples.

Outright "selling" the product or the business opportunity is the biggest mistake we see people make. You want people liking your posts, so you should post stories about your lifestyle and your accomplishments and travels in life. Make sure that these posts are not received as arrogant. Be tasteful in your posts and just share your life. Occasionally share other people's stories of results on the product and the business. We try and keep a good mix of real life sprinkled with business wins and product stories. This seems to keep people engaged and doesn't run them off. Lifestyle and fun pictures and videos attract people. Post things (lots of pictures and videos) that attract people and get them to "like." After all, we are in the business of attracting people!

We also spend a lot of time "liking" other peoples' posts so that they show up in our Newsfeed and we show up in theirs. We also occasionally reach out to others via private message to let them know what we are doing and see if they have an interest. Since we are more business driven than product driven, we tend to post more about lifestyle and traveling around. We live in a glass house and people watch. A lot of people that I talk to now know what's going on in my life. So much so, it kind of freaks me out!

Cindy: I love to watch who is on chat so I can message and chat with them. If I've had a personal relationship with them, I will chat with 'small talk' first. For example: How have you been? How are the kids? Are you still working in your (whatever their thing is). I ask those and other questions to get them to tell me what's going on in their life! Then, hopefully, they will start asking me similar questions, and I can tell them what I am doing, which leads into a conversation about my business. If I don't have a personal relationship with them, I will chat to ask them if they are open to watching a short video. If they are, I can send them a link on chat in hopes that they watch it right then!

Obstacles Overcome

Kirby: Over the 24 years we've been in network marketing, the biggest obstacle has been people. They're unpredictable and never cease to amaze me in the ones that let me down or disappoint us. But I've come to realize that this is just part of the business. It's a people business. The solution to this is to just keep bringing people on and not get hung up with those who disappoint you, those that don't get it and those that just want to complain or blame. It's been a personal growth journey for me, and as it turns out, that's also been one of the biggest benefits for me. It's about becoming a better person and helping others to do the same.

Cindy: Sometimes we want it more for people than they want it for themselves. We pour so much time into them and they really aren't committed and it turns out to be a waste of time. Keeping people focused and committed long enough to get their income growing is tough. Personal development is key to keeping them believing in themselves!

Meeting New People

Kirby: You've got to be likable and relatable. You've got to build rapport with people. It's true that, "They don't care how much you know until they know how much you care." You've got to find their pain point. What is their possible why? Why would they want to step out of their comfort zone and do this? Since we're focused on building a distribution network and the business side of it all, when we're talking to people, they usually quickly tell you that they don't like their job or they haven't had a vacation in years. With Facebook, if you've got a name and city, you can usually find them and find out all kinds of things about them.

Cindy: I met Tracy Jarvis while on a treadmill at the gym many years ago and recruited her into our first company. That turned out to be an interesting story since that is where she met Mark Jarvis. They married and, years later, started the company we distribute for. Now, we are two of their top consultants! When I meet someone while I am out and about, I think to myself, "This person could mean $10,000 a month to me if I speak to them. And if I don't, well, I will never know!"

Nurturing Relationships

Kirby: There is rapport-building. Then once you have a relationship, it becomes nurturing, but it's really all the same. It's about caring about their life and being an assertive listener.

Cindy: It's great to build friendships in the business. Some of my closest friends are in our company. But you also have to know when it's time for business and be able to discuss the business issues with them without them taking it personally!"

Continue To Learn

Congratulations on finishing this book! This is just the beginning of your next level of social media engagement. If you follow our advice, you'll go a long way. We recommend after reading through these pages that you read the book again, this time implementing everything we've recommended. Put a note in your calendar to review the book again in six months.

We are committed to helping you learn and to creating a positive and successful community of network marketers who get great Facebook results! If you have problems, don't give up! Reach out to us and let us know how you're doing and how we can help.

If you need more than the book... Bring the book to life with diagrams and how-to videos. Stay current with the latest changes in social media and how it can grow your business by joining our community:
http://socialmediadirectsales.com/training

We'd be honored to give you personal, one-on-one coaching. Go here to find out more:
http://socialmediadirectsales.com/coaching

Jim Lupkin & Brian Carter
November, 2014

About The Authors

Jim Lupkin, a 19-year veteran of network marketing and social media, has dedicated his career to applying the strategies found in this book. At the young age of 18, he joined his first network marketing company. Through his perseverance in overcoming failures, he learned to merge the online world with network marketing. He is the foremost authority on using social media to build a profitable network marketing business at the corporate and distributor level. His accomplishments have been covered by news media, including <u>Direct Selling News</u> magazine, <u>Inside Facebook</u> and <u>Inc.</u> magazine.

Brian Carter, a consultant, author and keynote speaker with 18 years of experience, is an international authority on how organizations can generate bigger business results with digital marketing. He is also the author of The Like Economy, Facebook Marketing, LinkedIn For Business, and The Cowbell Principle. Brian has developed marketing strategies and keynoted for companies of all sizes, including Microsoft, NBC, Universal Studios, The U.S. Army, The World Health Organization, PrideStaff and Dramamine. Brian has been interviewed by Bloomberg TV, The Wall Street Journal and Entrepreneur magazine.